The Mis-Adventures of Bus "94"

Author:
Samuel Thomas Mullis

A Short Storybook/Devotional
for Your Daily Enjoyment!
(Volume 1)

1

Copyright...

Copyright © 2023 Samuel Thomas Mullis

All rights reserved.

ISBN: 9798396968554

Opening Comments...

This is a short story book with simple chapters about the crazy things that have happened to me as a school bus driver as well as other "shared" short stories from other bus drivers. It is intended to be a devotional book. Anyone from age 15 to age 107 should be able to enjoy the content of this book, as it was purposefully written to be an easy read prior to bed or first thing in the morning. I have also provided meaningful and in most cases humorous clipart to accompany each story for added variety! I feel that it is a quick witted and entertaining book as well as thought provoking and you simply can't stop at one chapter, you will want to continue to read about each unique adventure and precarious situations I get myself into sometimes! I changed all names to protect the innocent as well as kept all schools and town in a vanilla context. Scriptural references are included that connect to each story. Bus drivers (in particular) from all across America can easily relate to these stories as this book has been created to reveal to any reader the crazy situations that all bus drivers may come across on any given day. The content of this book is timeless as it could happen to any driver anywhere and at any time! It could have happened yesterday, last week, last year, 30 years ago or even next week! It is entertaining to all even if you have never driven a bus or connected to the school system, you will find these short stories entertaining and insightful! I can guarantee you will have a smile and most likely laughter after reading these short stories! Enjoy!

4

Dedication...

I would like to take this opportunity to say thank you so very much to all the people who have encouraged me along the way to write this book. It has been a very long and tedious process. Special thanks to my sister: Sherrie Bailey for always being my anchor through the troubled times of life and spending hours of her personal time to proof read my book for grammatical errors, and making comments and suggestions. I also appreciate the kind support from my brother-in-law: Tim Bailey. Thanks also to my dad: Sherrill C. Mullis who has always been my personal hero and inspiration. He is 94 years young, and when I grow up, I want to be just like him. I also wish to acknowledge my deceased mother for being such a caring and prayerful person who was always encouraging me and telling me you can do it – don't give up! I wish to thank my sweet daughter Annabelle for her love and devotion and encouragement to me while creating my book(s). And finally, I wish to thank my Pastor, Reverend Barry Allen, for helping me to get this book published and showing me the ropes of how to navigate the publishing waters! Most of all thank you to God who is the Savior of my Life and without him none of this would be possible! Lastly, I would be remiss if I didn't give a shoutout to my bus driver family! As such, I wish to thank my fellow bus drivers that have supported my decisions and are such a sweet group of people to work with! I dedicate this book to my friends, family, and God!

Table of Contents...

Chapter 1 Get That Lizard Off Of My Foot!..9
Chapter 2 The Water Bottle Incident…..13
Chapter 3 The Penalty For Leaving A Child On The Bus! … 17
Chapter 4 The Fly on My Shoulder!..23
Chapter 5 The Dragon Foot Man! … 27
Chapter 6 There Is A Raccoon On My Bus!..33
Chapter 7 Queen Alexandra! … 37
Chapter 8 Seat Repair! Or So I Had Hoped… 41
Chapter 9 Pond Water Action Going On Here! …...............................47
Chapter 10 Take 'Em To The Wood Shed! 51
Chapter 11 A Prank I Did On A School Bus As A Student!.................55
Chapter 12 Body Piercing Needle On the Last Seat of the Bus!...........61
Chapter 13 Helping Another Bus Route Full Of Screamers!... 65
Chapter 14 My Bus Driver Adventures In High School! … 71
Chapter 15 The Dog That Rode My School Bus! ... .75
Chapter 16 Who Needs Google? I Have A Jenny-Jenny! … 79
Chapter 17 You Rat Fink!..83
Chapter 18 Hide Your Bus in the Wash Bay! ... .87
Chapter 19 Did You Pick Up Those Alibis yet?... 91
Chapter 20 I Don't Care, We Are Gonna Settle This Now!...................95
Chapter 21 An Unattended Toddler on the Curb!... 99
Chapter 22 Bob, Get Back to Your Seat and Sit Down!... 103
Chapter 23 Pluck Out Those Weeds, Smell Those Roses!..................107
Chapter 24 You Are Going To Become A School Teacher!................111

Chapter 25 That Cute Dimpled Smile…	115
Chapter 26 Slamming the Brakes Hurt My Kneecaps! …	119
Chapter 27 Don't Tell God His Breath Stinks!...	123
Chapter 28 The Spider Bite Parable…	127
Chapter 29 The Man that Owed 10,000 talents…	131
Chapter 30 I Give You a Piece of Me And A Prayer…	135
Chapter 31 Matty's Spider Bite Poison…	139
Chapter 32 Who's the B*t*h now, B*t*h?...	143
Chapter 33 Decisions You Make Today, Affects Your Future…	147
Chapter 34 Do You Still Have This Child on Your bus?...	151
Chapter 35 Both of You Are Right And Both Are Wrong…	157
Chapter 36 The Motorcycle Thugs I Refused to Trust…	161
Chapter 37 Their Justification for Their Actions…	165
Chapter 38 The Old Tree of Wisdom and Knowledge…	169
Chapter 39 The Bully and Mother Hijacking Scene…	173
Chapter 40 Texting While Driving Cost Me $$$...	177
Chapter 41 Johnny Farted…	183
Chapter 42 My typical day starts at 4:15 am…	187
Chapter 43 Cleanup on Row 5 Seat 7 – Hand Lotion…	193
Chapter 44 Imposter Student on My Bus…	196
Chapter 45 Poke Out Lips Girl…	200
Chapter 46 Insubordination…	204
Chapter 47 Suicide…	208
Chapter 48 Hey, KoolAid!...	212
Chapter 49 It's Friday and We Shall Treat It as Such!...	216
Chapter 50 Y'all Are Shining Like New Money!...	220
Chapter 51 Paradice!...	224

Chapter 52 Let's Get It!..228
Chapter 53 Easter Eggs! …..232
Chapter 54 Teddy Bear's Bus Was Hi-jacked!......................................236
Chapter 55 The Master Link…..240
Chapter 56 The Well-Oiled Machine…..244
Chapter 57 Foolish Horse-Play…..248
Chapter 58 Can You Say Busted?..252
Chapter 59 The Crazy Things You Find on a Bus…..........................256
Chapter 60 The Bus I Totaled in High School!..................................261
Stay Tuned! …..267

Chapter 1
Get That Lizard Off Of My Foot!...

Get that lizard off my foot! Get it off! Get it off! One day I was taking my Elementary kids home from school and kids were their typical noisy selves. One of my kindergarten kids began to scream out of pure terror to the top of his voice as he came running up the bus aisle to me. There was a bit of traffic behind me but I had no choice but to stop the bus and take care of the situation. Since this child was having a screaming episode, every child got up out of their seats and rushed to the front of the bus to see what was the matter with this child! It was utter chaos! Meanwhile, the other cars that were behind my bus grew concerned at the commotion they were seeing and hearing. One person got out of their car and wanted to know what all the commotion was about. The kids were screaming like someone was fighting or getting hurt and the driver got out of their car and came to the door to see what was going on! I quickly opened the door and explained it was an emergency issue that I had to tend to which caused all the kids to become unruly. I assured the person I had everything under control as I commanded the kids to go back to their assigned seats as the emergency was surely over. Gradually everyone's nerves settled down and I got everyone home safely. You will never guess what had happened to the kindergarten kid. You know kids love to chew candy and gum. Well, as soon as the kid come up to me with fear, panic, and trepidation all over him I snatched his shoe off his foot. He was screaming get it off! Get it off! Get that lizard off of me! It's hurting me! I couldn't help but chuckle when I discovered it was nothing more than a piece of sticky candy on the kid's shoe and he thought he was being bitten by a lizard!

Scripture of the day:

What does Scripture say about having pure fear?

God will give you strength when you are afraid. Its up to us to trust in and as I see it, it is also a genuine test of your faith. Do you completely rely on God through difficult times and hard situations?

Isaiah 41: 10 NIV

10 So do not fear, for I am with you; do not be dismayed, for I am your God. I will strengthen you and help you; I will uphold you with my righteous right hand.

Chapter 2
The Water Bottle Incident…

The water bottle incident was a situation where students had become so unruly on the bus that I had to intervene and take a stand and bust up the friend groups at the rear of the bus. I pulled into a parking space beside another bus. My bus has air conditioning… but for some reason the kids at the rear of the bus decided that they had to have the window down. Unbeknownst to me, the bus I pulled beside of opened their window and tossed in an open water bottle through the window. My students decided they wanted to retaliate and I was stuck in the middle trying to decide what the proper action was to take to make sure those actions did not go unpunished. Unfortunately, the cameras on my bus did not work and after writing up 13 people on my bus and complaining to the other bus driver about the whole incident (as she also had guilty parties involved as well) her cameras were also not working. The Principal told me he could not follow up on any type of intervention because there was no real proof of who did what. How frustrating to take the time to follow the proper protocol for situations such as this, and then no follow through or support given to discipline these students in this particular situation. I would also like to add the other driver did make an attempt to discipline her students involved as well but was facing the "proof" battle as well!

Scripture of the day:

What does Scripture say about undisciplined children?

Proverbs 13:24 NIV ... Whoever spares the rod hates their children, but the one who loves their children is careful to discipline them.

Proverbs 29:17 NIV Discipline your children, and they will give you peace; they will bring you the delights you desire.

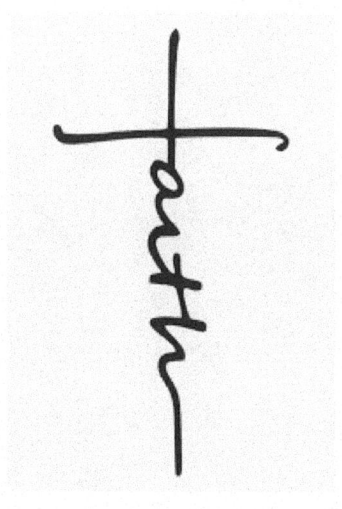

Chapter 3
The Penalty For Leaving A Child On The Bus! ...

Leaving a child on the bus cost a fellow driver his job for 4 days and about $800.00 of pay and remediation. I had a similar – yet different situation that happened to me. In addition to my normal duties, on this particular day, I took another route home in the afternoon to help out as the other driver was sick. To my amazement, that route was overpacked with 3 kids to every seat - all of them screaming! As a result of all the noise I missed a kid's stop because I couldn't hear him over all the chaotic noise by others on the bus! So, after I had finished most of the route, the remaining 6-7 children had to go to The Boys' and Girls' Club across town. I stopped and secured the bus and got out of my seat and moved each remaining student to a different seat and asked before I left for the other side of town if everyone else left on the bus was going to The Boys and Girls Club? They all shook their heads and said yes. After driving the 15-minute trip across town, I arrived at The Boys and Girls Club. Most kids got off the bus to go inside, however; this one kid says "Hey you missed my stop!" I asked him "What do you mean I missed your stop? I didn't miss your stop because I stopped at every stop on the route description – you just didn't get off the bus!" He said "I think I was asleep when you got to my stop!" (I'm pretty sure he just was not paying attention when I was delivering students to their stops in his community). I was absolutely furious! I called out on the radio to see if there might be another driver that was in the area that was headed back across town. By God's grace another driver was in the vicinity and indeed was headed back close to where the student lived at. The kid boarded the other driver's bus and I was so thankful! The next morning when I arrived for work, there was a writeup in my box for a safety violation! It was a safety violation for leaving a sleeping child on my bus (unattended) and not checking for sleepers! But I never actually left the kid alone(unattended) on my bus, I was with him on the bus the entire time! I had to plead my case to the boss. When he discovered I never actually left the kid on the bus, all was forgiven. A day or so later another one of my supervisors explained to me that another driver had got suspended from duty because he actually had left a kid (unknowingly) sleeping on the bus for an hour or so after he had finished his morning run. The driver got off his bus - leaving the sleeping kid behind and unattended (of course unknowingly). A few hours later, the driver went through his pre-trip bus inspection procedures and discovered the sleeping kid on the bus! My other Supervisor said he almost got fired because of it! I normally always check after every run and procedures dictate that I have to go to the rear of the bus to depress the reset button at the rear of the bus, but I don't just rely on the reset button. I make sure I check each seat as I travel to the back of the bus to hit that reset button. You may like to know it's a pretty good safety feature that forces all drivers to go to the rear of the bus to hit reset, if they fail to press the reset button and they open the door to leave the bus, the

PLEASE DO NOT LEAVE CHILDREN UNATTENDED

honking horn alarm will go off to remind them if they had checked the bus for sleeping students. This is very embarrassing if you forget! Safety of the children is most important!

Scripture of the day:

What does Scripture say about people who judge you?

Matthew 7:1-5 NIV

1 "Do not judge, or you too will be judged. 2 For in the same way you judge others, you will be judged, and with the measure you use, it will be measured to you. 3 "Why do you look at the speck of sawdust in your brother's eye and pay no attention to the plank in your own eye? 4 How can you say to your brother, 'Let me take the speck out of your eye,' when all the time there is a plank in your own eye? 5 You hypocrite, first take the plank out of your own eye, and then you will see clearly to remove the speck from your brother's eye.

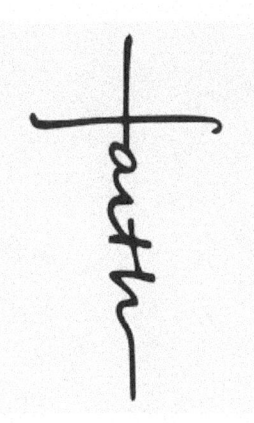

Chapter 4
The Fly on My Shoulder!...

The fly on my shoulder is a method of dealing with bullies. Often, parents can be clueless as to what we have to deal with daily on the school bus – especially with Elementary kids who refuse to abide by the pre-established rules on the bus that are posted! Some parents complain they want their 1st grade child at the front of the bus because they have been told by their daughter or son that the older kids are bullying them. But the problem is those 1st grade kids are equally as bad as the older kids and sometimes are the very ones who are causing the issues! Landon and Kinley had fought each other on the bus once before, so that means that I have to keep those two kids separated and not sitting anywhere close to one another. Meanwhile, Landon not only is bullying Kinley 5 seats away, but he is also threatening to fight an older kid. The older kid told me he (Landon) starts all that at the bus stop before they even load the bus! I sat down with Kinley and explained to him that the best way to deal with bullies is to ignore them and pretend they are a fly on your shoulder and thump them off! Don't say anything back to them to retaliate because once you do… then they in turn must say something back and you say something back to them and then a potential fight breaks out. Also, the potential exists of getting suspended from school when it's not even your fault. If you can ignore them then that is the smarter move! Kinley looked at me with his long blond hair and blue eyes… and said "Ok Mr. Sam I might try that and see what happens!"

Scripture of the day:

What does Scripture say about having arguments?

God's Word tells us specifically to avoid arguments as expressed in this scripture…

2 Timothy 2:23-24 NIV

23 Don't have anything to do with foolish and stupid arguments, because you know they produce quarrels. 24 And the Lord's servant must not be quarrelsome but must be kind to everyone, able to teach, not resentful.

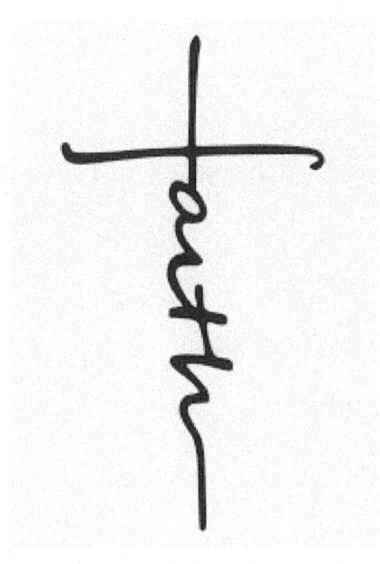

Chapter 5
The Dragon
Foot Man! ...

The dragon foot man... Upon leaving the bus depot (especially in the afternoon there is always a patron in the community – that seems to be homeless to me – or at the very least something not quite right in his mind!) He is a "dragon foot man" with what appears to be a peg leg dragging his way in the middle of the road, yes, the middle of the lane you are driving in! He doesn't care anything about his own safety! He drags that lame leg beside him and walks most everywhere he goe. I have heard a lot of other drivers complaining about him saying "There goes dragon leg again watch out for him! What's his problem – How come he can't walk on the sidewalk like a normal person?" One driver that was actually related to him said that's just the way he be? Someone asked, "Is he homeless?" Another driver said "No he's got a home he's just touched in the head and chooses to walk the streets like that – he's always been like that!" So, I'm thinking to my-self, and yes at first, I sort of judged him my-self in the negative. But after seeing him and hearing others voice similar opinions, I got to thinking well maybe I ...meaning myself... (as well as other drivers) should be thankful that we are not in his mental prison! How would you like to have to walk a mile, much less 10 steps in his shoes? None of us know the torment he has to mentally endure! Why do you judge him? Why can't we just be happy and pray for him that nothing bad happens to him. He obviously doesn't care that you are on the road. We should be thankful we are not in his mental state of mind! So, from here on every time I see him, I say a special prayer that God will take care of him and continue to protect him in his fragile state of mind!

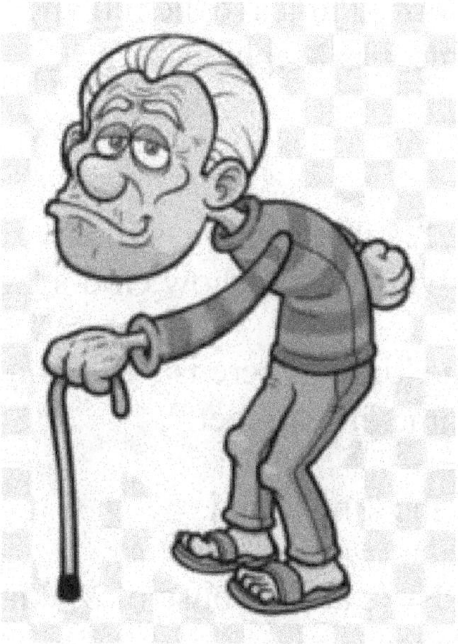

Scripture of the day:

What does Scripture say about a cripple person?

2 Samuel 4:4 NIV and 2 Samuel 9:3-9 NIV

2 Samuel 4:4 NIV

4 Jonathan son of Saul had a son who was lame in both feet. He was five years old when the news about Saul and Jonathan came from Jezreel. His nurse picked him up and fled, but as she hurried to leave, he fell and became disabled. His name was Mephibosheth.

2 Samuel 9:3-9 NIV

3The king asked, "Is there no one still alive from the house of Saul to whom I can show God's kindness?"

Ziba answered the king, "There is still a son of Jonathan; he is lame in both feet."

4"Where is he?" the king asked.

Ziba answered, "He is at the house of Makir son of Ammiel in Lo Debar."

5 So King David had him brought from Lo Debar, from the house of Makir son of Ammiel.

6When Mephibosheth son of Jonathan, the son of Saul, came to David, he bowed down to pay him honor.

David said, "Mephibosheth!"

"At your service," he replied.

7 "Don't be afraid," David said to him, "for I will surely show you kindness for the sake of your father Jonathan. I will restore to you all the land that belonged to your grandfather Saul, and you will always eat at my table."

8 Mephibosheth bowed down and said, "What is your servant, that you should notice a dead dog like me?"

9 Then the king summoned Ziba, Saul's steward, and said to him, "I have given your master's grandson everything that belonged to Saul and his family. [10] You and your sons and your servants are to farm the land for him and bring in the crops, so that your master's grandson may be provided for. And Mephibosheth, grandson of your master, will always eat at my table."

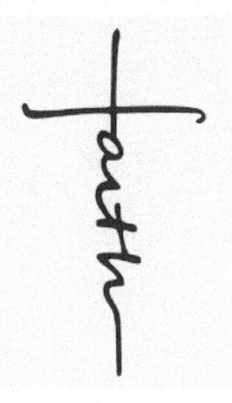

Chapter 6
There Is A Raccoon On My Bus!...

There is a raccoon on my bus! One day at the beginning of the year, we had a safety meeting. The safety Boss was stressing to us the importance of checking our bus very thoroughly during the pre-trip inspection. He showed us a video from a bus camera. The lady had finished doing her morning pre-inspection check and got behind the wheel and was actually driving. While she was driving, she looked down at her feet and screamed "Oh Lord Sweet Jesus!" Luckily, she was a seasoned driver and it was before picking up anyone. She pulled her bus over and you could see a racoon exiting off the bus! Obviously, it was the racoon's first day to ride a school bus and he was just amazed as she was! The safety Boss said when you get on your bus as part of your inspection make sure that you walk that aisle and make sure no critters have crawled their way onto your bus! What if that was a rabid racoon? What if there were kids on that bus? You just can't be too safe! Always be cognizant not only of your surroundings but also of what's inside your bus too! Make sure you close your door at the end of the day and close your hatches and windows to prevent such occurrences as this!

Scripture of the day:

What does Scripture say about animals that seem to be demon possessed? The person on the bus that encountered the raccoon I am sure thought that raccoon was demon possessed!

Matthew 8:28-34 NIV

28 When he arrived at the other side in the region of the Gadarenes, two demon-possessed men coming from the tombs met him. They were so violent that no one could pass that way. 29 "What do you want with us, Son of God?" they shouted. "Have you come here to torture us before the appointed time?" 30 Some distance from them a large herd of pigs was feeding. 31 The demons begged Jesus, "If you drive us out, send us into the herd of pigs." 32 He said to them, "Go!" So they came out and went into the pigs, and the whole herd rushed down the steep bank into the lake and died in the water. 33 Those tending the pigs ran off, went into the town and reported all this, including what had happened to the demon-possessed men. 34 Then the whole town went out to meet Jesus. And when they saw him, they pleaded with him to leave their region.

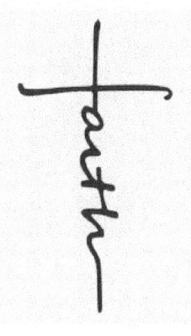

Chapter 7
Queen Alexandra! ...

I have a student on my bus - let's call her Queen Alexandra. She has ridden my bus for 2 years. When she first started riding my bus, she was such a charming and sweet girl. She was aways very polite and kind to me. I always greet every student every day with a good morning so and so! I suppose she was a typical girl, pretty, long hair and enjoyed flirting with the boys. She bounced from one boy on the bus to another with shall we call it relationships. One day she had to make a statement and got on the bus and was all cuddled up with a guy on the bus and I just felt like that was so inappropriate. I busted up their seating arrangements and told them there had to be a minimum of 6 rows of seats between them. She was irately furious – so much so that she got on the bus and cradled the dudes face and said I just love you so much and kissed him on the mouth. I was livid! When I got to her stop at the end of the route, I explained to her that her behavior was not appropriate for a school bus. It was not my job to be a chauffer for her and her boyfriend to be on a date on the school bus. That was one reason why I had separated their seating assignments and this kissing business was totally out of the question. Eventually, the boy ended up moving to Florida with his parents and then kids knew she went with 2-3 different boys on the bus and sadly they ended up not having much to do with her. Somewhere along the way she decided that I made her feel uncomfortable when I was around her. So, she said for future reference I don't like it when you are around me because you make me feel uncomfortable. But every time

I looked up in my rear-view mirror to check on student behavior, she was either staring at me or she had a camera taking a video of me. There are already cameras on the bus. I am very careful about what I do or say to students. The day she told me she felt uncomfortable around me, she was eating chips. I told her ok since you continue to choose to be rude to me when you get on the bus and in the middle of my good morning greeting you interrupt me to say Good morning to the girl behind me then you can't eat food or have drinks on my bus! Its clearly in the rules posted on the bus and it is up to my discretion as to how I choose to enforce those rules. A few days later she walks on the bus with a large fountain drink in her hand. I told her 3 times to get rid of it. She chose not to so I wrote her up and also submitted a copy of the bus rules that are clearly posted on the bus! Of course, she got in trouble and was irate. Since out little talk, I totally look the opposite way when she gets on the bus. I greet the 2 other students that get on the bus and when she gets on or off, I totally ignore her and refuse to make any eye contact whatsoever with her – but I'm my normal friendly bus driver self towards the other students! So. the last day of school she decided she is going to have the last laugh. She brings a cake plate full of chocolate cupcakes giving them out to her friends on the bus. I was furious but I totally ignored it and said nothing. It was after-all the last day of school! So, the next school year I suppose the drama will continue because she was NOT a senior.

Scripture of the day:

What does Scripture say about people that think they are better than their peers?

Romans 12:3-5 NIV

Humble Service in the Body of Christ

3 For by the grace given me I say to every one of you: Do not think of yourself more highly than you ought, but rather think of yourself with sober judgment, in accordance with the faith God has distributed to each of you. 4 For just as each of us has one body with many members, and these members do not all have the same function, 5 so in Christ we, though many, form one body, and each member belongs to all the others.

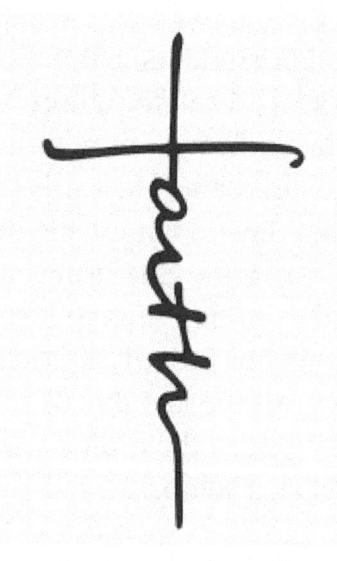

Chapter 8
Seat Repair! Or So I Had Hoped…

One of our duties as a bus driver is to report rips and tears of seats on the bus. We have a person that will come out and repair the seats with new seat covers. The mechanic told me he didn't have enough material in stock to do the repair job. So the repair got postponed. We had agreed upon another date and time to get my seats repaired but at the last minute I was called to help out with another shuttle bus run. He said "Ok, I guess we will have to reschedule your repairs to another date." Well one day led to a week, which lead to a 2nd week, then a third week and before I knew it the problem grew from not only a tear on one seat but now it had grown into a giant tear, plus two more seats within the same area were getting in bad shape too! The mechanic and I discussed the repair once again. He said, "Well this is the third time you have asked me about it! Every time we schedule it to be repaired it seems like something comes up and it doesn't get done. But we will get it tended to because I can see its getting much worse than when we started about a month ago!" I was so thankful when we managed to find a date where both of us were available and there were adequate materials available to do the repair! The mechanic was actually also another driver with the school system – who happened (as a benefit to our school system) the necessary skills to perform the seat repairs.

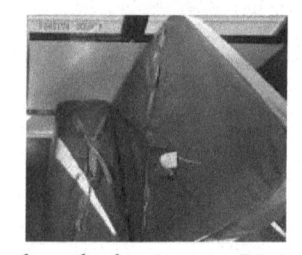

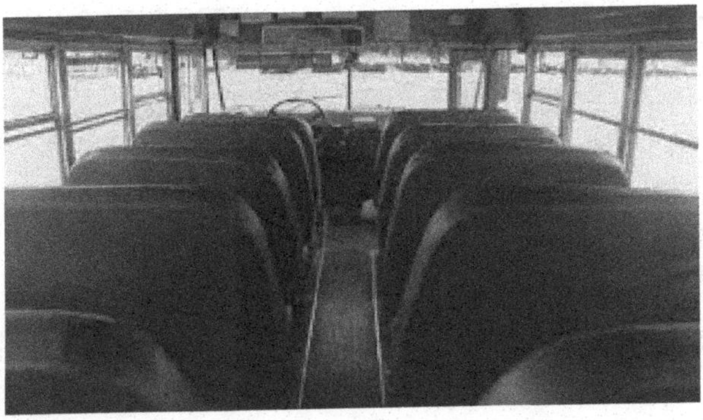

Scripture of the day:

What does Scripture say about resource management?

After a google search, these are the comments I discovered pertinent to the question that are noteworthy:

The Bible is full of passages instructing us to use our resources to care for the poor and those who are in need… (1 **John 3:17–18, Proverbs 28:27, 1 Timothy 5:8**). Stewardship isn't about "giving back" to God. It's about using what he's given us to accomplish something that matters.

1 John 3:17–18 NIV

17 If anyone has material possessions and sees a brother or sister in need but has no pity on them, how can the love of God be in that person? 18 Dear children, let us not love with words or speech but with actions and in truth.

Proverbs 28:27 NIV

27 Those who give to the poor will lack nothing, but those who close their eyes to them receive many curses.

1 Timothy 5:8 NIV

8 Anyone who does not provide for their relatives, and especially for their own household, has denied the faith and is worse than an unbeliever.

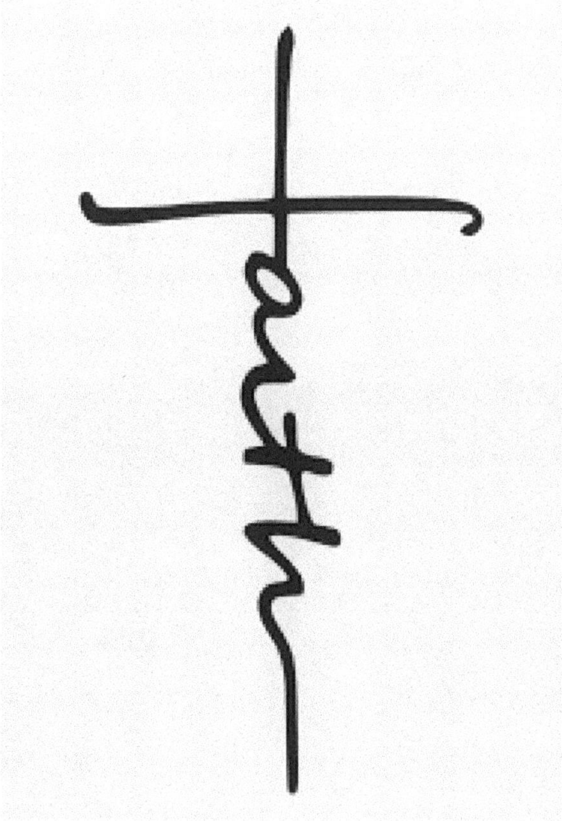
faith

Chapter 9
Pond Water Action Going On Here! ...

Pond Water Action. I have grown very fond to hear some of the jargon that is used on the road to describe poor driving behaviors of other people on the road. We all have come across situations while driving. Always without fail, it occurs when you are in a hurry - that dreaded slow stop-light catches you, or someone is crossing the street; and, dare I say it… because you know it has also happened to you when you were in a hurry! … a darn old school bus is stopping… and even worse than that it is a handicapped bus where you have to wait even longer for them to let the ramp down to load the student on the bus and then wait until they raise the ramp and secure the kid and then (or so it seems) they are never in a hurry to get to their destination! Well, it also happens to school bus drivers – especially when we are doing a shuttle run. We inevitably get behind (usually – but not always) an elderly person who doesn't have a care in this world creeping along usually in their safety zone of 10 mph below the acceptable speed limit! So, one day as I was travelling, I heard "POND WATER!..." come across the radio. When I got back to the bus depot, I inquired from the bus driver what he meant by that…. He went on to explain to me – well haven't you ever been around pond water? It's stale and not moving and stagnant… so sometimes I get behind slow drivers and they remind me of Pond water! I laughed so much I nearly cried!

Scripture of the day:

What does Scripture say about having to wait on other people?

James 5:7-11 NIV

Patience in Suffering

7 Be patient, then, brothers and sisters, until the Lord's coming. See how the farmer waits for the land to yield its valuable crop, patiently waiting for the autumn and spring rains. 8 You too, be patient and stand firm, because the Lord's coming is near. 9 Don't grumble against one another, brothers and sisters, or you will be judged. The Judge is standing at the door! 10 Brothers and sisters, as an example of patience in the face of suffering, take the prophets who spoke in the name of the Lord. 11 As you know, we count as blessed those who have persevered. You have heard of Job's perseverance and have seen what the Lord finally brought about. The Lord is full of compassion and mercy.

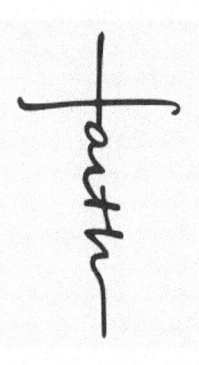

Chapter 10
Take 'Em To The Wood Shed! ...

Take 'em to the Wood Shed! Of all things to come across the radio! Once again, I had to inquire from my mentor shuttle bus driver what he meant by "woodshed." The "shout-out" came when another driver called for assistance from an administrator – once they arrived at school. When you hear that (as a fellow bus-driver) you know someone is having to hassle with a discipline issue or worse than that a fight on their bus. So, I asked my mentor friend what he meant by "woodshed." He is an older man and apparently had parents that spared the rod NOT to spoil the child! My mentor told me: well, when you showed out when you were a child, what did your parents do to you? I told him I got a whooping' My mentor said Yep there you go! You're on the right idea! When I was young and I got out of line my daddy took me out to the woodshed and tore my tail up…. Mostly with his belt, or whatever he could put his hands on. My grandma told me to go pull off a switch from the Cherry tree and she said it better be a good one too – I ain't talking about no twig either! So, I totally agree, some of these kids need to have a personal visit to the woodshed and if there were more whoopings (or more severe punishments) for kids giving us problems on the bus, we wouldn't have the discipline issues we deal with on a daily basis. I totally agree! Woodshed!!!

Scripture of the Day:

What does Scripture have to say about spanking children?

Proverbs 13:24 NIV

24 Whoever spares the rod hates their children, but the one who loves their children is careful to discipline them.

Proverbs 29:15-17 NIV

15 A rod and a reprimand impart wisdom, but a child left undisciplined disgraces its mother. 16 When the wicked thrive, so does sin, but the righteous will see their downfall. 17 Discipline your children, and they will give you peace; they will bring you the delights you desire.

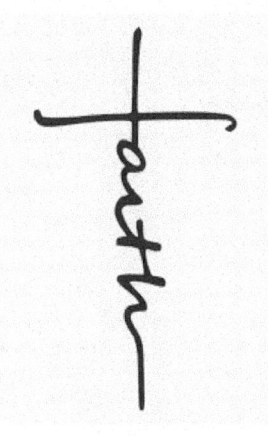

Chapter 11
A Prank I Did On A School Bus As A Student!...

You know, I'm not sure why it happens but it seems that when you are in High School there always has to be some sort of prank you have to play on another unsuspecting friend! Maybe you can recall a prank you played on someone during your High School years? Anyway, I had two buddies in High School who were also coincidentally School Bus drivers just like me! I'll call them Ricky and Jefferson. One late night my Buddy Ricky said let's go over to Jefferson's house and roll his bus! Me, being the gullible person I was who always was supposed to know better than to hang around anyone who would get me in trouble, inquired - How the heck are we gonna do that? It's way too heavy for me and you to lift! My so-called friend loved to make a fool out of you and took every opportunity to point out your shortcomings. He said no, you idiot, I don't mean to roll over the bus I mean roll it with toilet paper. It's a harmless prank and tomorrow morning when Jefferson gets up at 5 am to do his morning run(s) and goes outside to crank up his bus to get it warm, there will be toilet paper all over it! Won't that be so funny? I didn't see too much harm in doing the prank, so reluctantly, I agreed to go along and dare I say it, I even participated in it too. So, Jefferson parked his bus at his parent's house. There was a small vacant lot of woods between his house and an appliance store. I drove a 1976 Chevy panel van which was my dad's truck he used in his door-to-door salesman business. I was thankful to have any kind of wheels (much less a fancy car) that I could drive back and forth to and from school and be cool enough to not have to ride the school bus (or even worst, have my parents to take me to and from school). At least that was the case until I actually started driving the bus at school during my 10th - 12th grade years. Anyway, we parked the car late at night on a Sunday, went through the vacant wooded lot to roll his bus. Ricky always had a mean streak. He also brought along with him a dozen eggs and a can of sardines! I asked him, "Hey what is all that for?" He said, "We're not only gonna roll his bus but we are also gonna egg it and put sardines on the motor so they will stink when the motor gets hot!" We were already there in the heat of the moment adrenaline kicking in because we knew if we got caught, we would be in some serious trouble. To this day I know I hesitated to participate because I knew better, but Ricky convinced me that it was harmless fun, and that one day, when we were old men, we could tell our grandkids about the crazy things we did as teenagers when we were in high school. I knew I was always taught to be pretty straight laced, and not get in any trouble, but I figured ok well, I'll do this one time and never again. Did I mention Ricky had a mean streak? Well, he proceeded to toss the eggs behind the seats at the rear of the bus and put the sardines on the motor. Then just before we left to go back to my dad's van, he said wait there's one more thing we gotta do…. I rebutted… well don't you think we have done enough already? Now Jefferson was a rather large kid, so, Ricky brought a 2X4 and jammed the rear door shut with the 2X4. Then he went to the front of the bus and slammed the door shut so the only way to get on the bus was to crawl through the driver's window – which there was no way our "friend" could fit! He said we are gonna laugh till we cry when Jefferson is running 20 minutes late on his route tomorrow morning because he can't get in the bus to start it! I (somewhat unwillingly) agreed but I sure did feel bad about the whole situation. In fact, after that prank I was thinking it was so cruel to be so mean to someone when I was taught to know right from wrong and this was totally against my better judgement. I never participated on any more pranks after that. As fate would have it, (you know sometimes karma comes up to bite you) the end of this story gets a unique twist. I think our buddy was late on his route and pretty pissed about the eggs and sardines. He said he had to wake up his older brother Randy (who was skinny as a bone) to go squeeze through the driver's window and get on that bus. When we walked back through the woods to get back to my dad's van parked at the appliance store parking lot the sheriff patrol was waiting there when we exited the woods! They were on patrol and a panel van backed up to an appliance store just looked awful suspicious to them! Luckily Ricky had the gift of gab and a talented tongue and he said with such a polished and respectful Voice…well officer, this is my friend's dad's van. We just came by for a visit with a friend who lives on the other side of this patch of woods. We come here often to see him but there is no where we can park our cars so we had to park here in this parking lot. My heart was pounding! I prayed, Oh dear God, I promise I will never ever do another foolish thing like this again if you get me out of this situation! To my amazement God heard my prayer. The Sherriff's Officer said "Ok boys, well can you see from our point of view how suspicious it appears? It looks like someone is trying to steal appliances from this store with a big chevy van backed up to the building like this!" Somehow, by the grace of God, he let us go! I was so thankful!

Scripture of the Day:

What does Scripture have to say about playing a prank(s) on your neighbor?

Proverbs 26: 18-21 NIV

18 Like a maniac shooting flaming arrows of death 19 is one who deceives their neighbor and says, "I was only joking!" 20 Without wood a fire goes out; without a gossip a quarrel dies down. 21 As charcoal to embers and as wood to fire, so is a quarrelsome person for kindling strife.

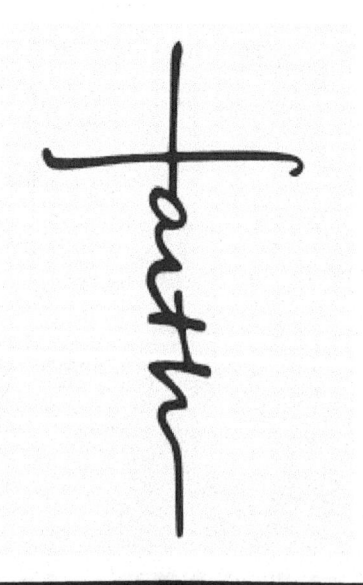

Chapter 12
Body Piercing Needle On the Last Seat of the Bus!

Sometimes as bus drivers we run across the craziest things on the bus. Part of our duties is to keep our buses clean. We are suppose to wash the outside ever so often, and mop the inside. Daily, we are supposed to pick up the trash off the floors and sweep out from under the seats. One day a fellow bus driver came across the radio and said I want my tapes pulled. I just found a thick gauge needle at the back of my bus and even worse than that there is blood all over the back seat! Upon further investigation of the video tapes a High School girl performed "surgery" on a Middle School girl and apparently pierced her belly button for her! I am absolutely amazed at how kids think they are so invincible at a young age doing things like this. All the girls saw was I want to wear some body jewelry in my belly button so I can be "Cool!" But they didn't stop to think what would happen once they did the piercing about the bleed out! There was blood all over the seat. The bus driver went through the appropriate protocol procedures and wrote up both girls for their actions. The principals of both the High School and the Middle school appropriately suspended both girls for two weeks from riding the bus. To my amazement, a few days later my bus driver friend called out to dispatch asking why were these girls were standing at the bus stop when they were supposed to still be on suspension? Dispatch told her, take them on to school and come by the office, we will explain a bit later on today. Curiosity was about to get the best of me! So, I asked my friend, "What did Dispatch tell her?" She said the parents went before the school board and got the principals' decision reversed. They only stayed suspended for 3 days instead of the 2 weeks. That's exactly what is wrong with society today!...Absolutely NO Accountability!

Scripture(s) of the day:

What does Scripture have to say about body piercing(s)?

Leviticus 19:28 NIV.

28 "'Do not cut your bodies for the dead or put tattoo marks on yourselves. I am the Lord.

1 Corinthians 6:19-20 NIV

19 Do you not know that your bodies are temples of the Holy Spirit, who is in you, whom you have received from God? You are not your own; 20 you were bought at a price. Therefore honor God with your bodies.

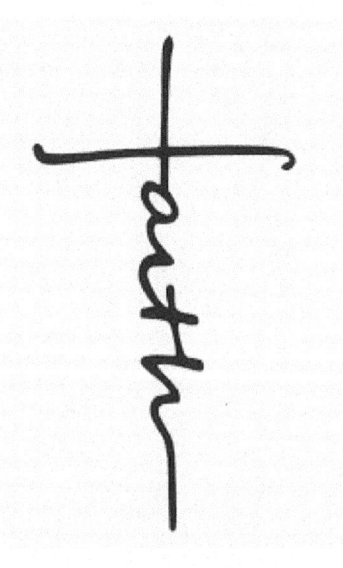

Chapter 13
Helping Another Bus Route Full Of Screamers!...

The Screaming Bus Route. From time to time, we are asked to help out with other bus drivers' routes when they have an unexpected emergency situation come up. Those kids still need transportation to and from school. So, I agreed to help out. It was a little bit of a challenge to learn the route but learning the route was absolutely the LEAST of my worries. Generally speaking, kids are not too bad in the morning because they are still sleepy and are not amped up on candy and such. But in the afternoon, it is an entirely different ballgame! These kids were wall to wall - 3 kids to a seat and the bus was packed out full. Every time I went over a bump, they screamed to the top of their voice and giggled and just thought it was a real roller coaster ride. So, on this particular day on the trip home while they were so unruly, I thought I had a good idea! I decided to stop the bus and wait for them to settle down and get quiet! I told them "I can wait right here as long as I need to because I am getting paid by the hour, (obviously not revealing to them I have other runs and other duties that needed to be tended to in addition to substitute driving their bus route) so we can just sit here in this hot bus and when you get quiet we will leave. I refuse to move this bus until you get quiet! Problem solved! (…or so I thought) Actually it was the beginning of a disaster. They were quiet for maybe 15 seconds but not only did they not get quiet they actually got even louder than before! When I called on the radio to tell Dispatch I was taking them back to school because of their unruly behavior Dispatch's response was no one is at the school, and it's too late in the day to turn around and go back to school so you gotta do whatever it takes and get them home! I was not a happy camper! Then, to my amazement, at the end of the day, Dispatch told me I had to help with that route indefinitely until they could hire another driver for that route! It only took about 25 minutes to get them home but it was 25 minutes of "pure top of their lungs screaming torture!" I am not one to be defeated easily! So, one day I discovered a pretty decent solution. I noticed one of the older girls was really the true instigator and she and her band of friends were the root cause of most of the noise issues. So, I sat that older girl by herself and would not allow any of her friends to sit beside her or near her. She was mad at me but the noise level got cut out by about 75%! Eventually all the kids gained respect for me because she was the root of all evil and they saw how I reacted towards her bad behavior and got the point… Wow, this driver don't play and he means business!

Scripture of the day:

What does the Scripture say about staying calm in chaos?

Philippians 4:6-7 NIV

6 Do not be anxious about anything, but in every situation, by prayer and petition, with thanksgiving, present your requests to God. 7 And the peace of God, which transcends all understanding, will guard your hearts and your minds in Christ Jesus.

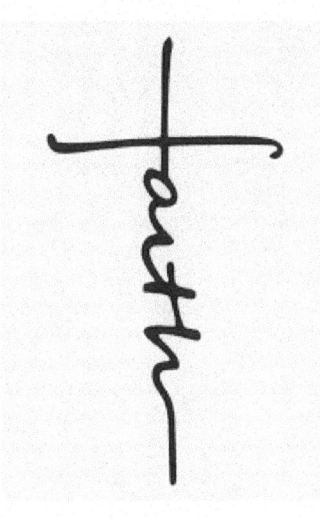

Chapter 14
My Bus Driver Adventures In High School! ...

One of the privileges of being a student in High School was being able to be distinguished as a student bus driver. I took training at the encouragement of a close friend of mine, and the icing on the cake was when he told me that chicks dig guys who drive school buses! So, of course, I signed up for the rather rigorous training and it, and before long until I found myself behind the wheel. Unfortunately, not really catching any chicks, but I sure did enjoy the accolades and pride of being one of the few "elite" student bus drivers! Another proud moment of a bus driver was getting a letterman's jacket like a football or basketball player would wear. Of course, this made the jocks rather jealous because they said all we did was pay money for our jackets but in our own sort of way (via the training and bus driving boot camp we had to go through a lot and felt we had an elite comradery…) I even paid an extra $30.00 to have my last name on the back of my jacket! I was so proud of my new "status symbol" Now all those chicks could see who I was from far away! The coat was the school colors – a royal blue with gold letters embroidered across the back of it. But after all that, I only had one girl that ever said much of anything about it and we never went out! I drove bus 7 and my buddy drove 12 and he'd say in class – Yoh 7 Who 'ya going out with this weekend? I just sort of shrugged and told him "Well, how about you take a few chicks from your harem and cripple them up so maybe I can catch me one or two!"

Scripture of the Day:

What does Scripture have to say about flirting with women?

Exodus 20:17

17 "You shall not covet your neighbor's house. You shall not covet your neighbor's wife, or his male or female servant, his ox or donkey, or anything that belongs to your neighbor."

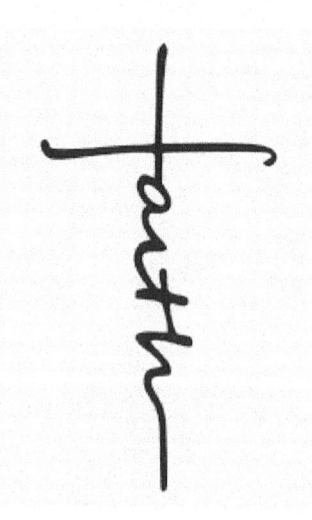

Chapter 15
The Dog That Rode My School Bus! ...

A dog riding to school on a bus? Back in the day, I always loved animals and someone had given me a Labrador retriever dog. But the dog seemed "tetched in the head." When I walked up to pet the dog (of course his tail was waggin' because he was always happy to see me!) His entire body would wiggle waggle and when I walked up to him, he would look at me like there were two of me! I made a joke of it and told my buddies I named the dog "C'mere Stay." And every time I walked up to him, I was trying to train him to stay at one spot but I called him c'mere stay and it just drove him crazy! He didn't know if he was coming or staying! But seriously I think something happened to him when he got in a fight one time with my buddy's dog on a hunting trip… My buddy's dog was part pit bull dog and when we arrived at our destination my buddy's dog got into a fight with him. My crazy dog also hated storms and lightning. He would always whimper and cry to get inside. I'm not sure if he ran away due to a storm or just exactly what happened to him. Anyway, one day I was driving and saw a lab strolling in the community. My dog's real name was Smokey Joe. I drove past him and thought to myself… "Hey that looks like my dog but he's been gone for several weeks! I stopped and opened the door and I yelled out… Hey

Smokey Joe, come here boy… " Clickity click, he smiles really big with tongue waggling and jumped right up in the 1st seat of the bus ready for me to take him to school or take him anywhere. It became obvious to me this was not my older dog but we bonded instantly. We took out an advertisement in the local newspaper… Lost dog found but nobody claimed him. He went on to become the family pet a good 12-15 years after that!

Scripture of the day:

What does scripture say about being kind to animals?

The response as ascertained from a google search about common questions people ask revealed the following:

Kindness to animals is godly. In fact, caring for them is part of our purpose.

Proverbs 12:10 NIV

10 The righteous care for the needs of their animals,
    but the kindest acts of the wicked are cruel.

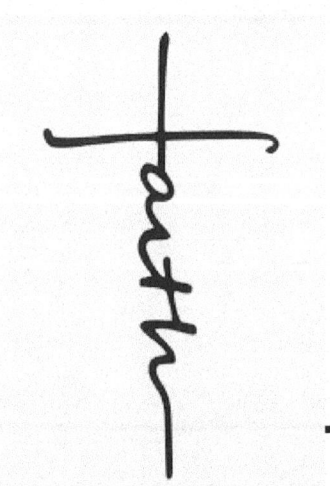

Chapter 16
Who Needs Google? I Have A Jenny-Jenny! ...

Sometimes you can hear the craziest things on the radio! And there is always ample opportunity for everyone that thinks they know everything there is to know about life and they are quick not only to give you advice on what you should do in any given situation but also how to do it. Well sometimes the "newbies can have a tendency to get lost in their directions. To the average person, they think how hard could this job be? A monkey could do our job! But consider this… place yourself behind the wheel of this school bus that you know how to operate but just barely because you are new at it. Then suppose you had to learn a new route and were placed in an area that you are totally unfamiliar with. Yes you have turn by turn instructions but what happens when one or two of the instructions out of about 6 pages of directions has the wrong turn on it or is just a simple mistake! Then dispatch is calling you to ask if you missed a stop which you did because the directions are wrong. Fortunately instead of the old "Tom-tom" navigators that you could punch in an address and it would tell you turn by turn how to get there from here, nowadays we can use the app "Google Maps." Well, who needs that when you have a fellow driver to call out on the radio – in her case Jenny who tells you… turn right on Hilcrest, left on Stevens, right at the light… go about a mile and the house is on the left with a red door and a white picket fence around it, you can't miss it! Mind you that you are obviously multitasking as you are following directions on the radfio, while Johnny is pulling Peggy's hair who is screaming to them STOP and other kids are giggling and laughing and talking extremely loud. Thus you can barely even hear what is on the radio… now YOU (or anyone for that matter) try to drive and multitask under those conditions!

Scripture of the day:

What does Scripture say about God guiding and directing your path?

Proverbs 3:5-6 NIV

5 Trust in the Lord with all your heart and lean not on your own understanding; 6 in all your ways submit to him, and he will make your paths straight.

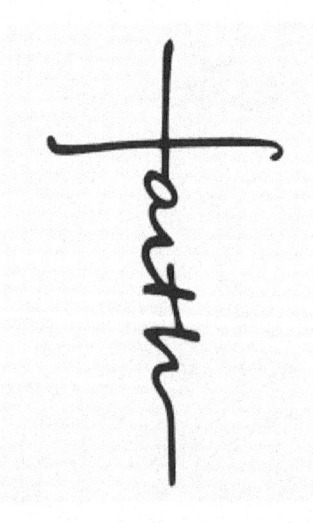

Chapter 17
You Rat Fink!...

You rat fink for calling out other drivers! As a freshman driver we are trained to follow the rules we were taught in training and on occasion older veterans have been known to point out the "Error" of our ways. Although it always made me mad when people pointed out my mistakes… eventually I embraced what they were saying and became a much better bus driver because of it. On this particular day a bus driver passed me on the right side. It's illegal for a bus to pass another school bus – pretty much like running through a stop light illegally. Anyway, I called it out on the radio… the other driver expressed her displeasure at me calling out her mistake over the radio. Once I got to the High School another driver who had heard the transmission also radioed in, and told me that was a big No-No. You should never call out another driver's mistakes over the radio, it makes you a rat fink! You shouldn't do stuff like that over the radio. Once I got my students off-loaded at the high school, I noticed his bus was parked there and so I walked over to his bus to discuss the issues with him. I explained to him that being called out on the radio was how I learned from MY mistakes when someone else pointed them out to me. Yes, I was embarrassed when they did it over the radio, so I made sure I asked questions from some of the veteran drivers to find out what I was doing wrong so I could fix it! My fellow bus driver had an opposite opinion, and after the smoke of the argument had blown over, (I don't like my bus family to be mad at me), so I told him well, I totally disagree with your viewpoint, but

I don't want any other of my bus-driver family to be mad at me so from now on I'll just keep my mouth shut!

Scripture of the day:

What does Scripture say about correcting others?

Here are a few scripture verses that teach us how to correct one another in love:

Galatians 6:1-6 NIV

Brothers and sisters, if someone is caught in a sin, you who live by the Spirit should restore that person gently. But watch yourselves, or you also may be tempted. [2] Carry each other's burdens, and in this way you will fulfill the law of Christ. [3] If anyone thinks they are something when they are not, they deceive themselves. [4] Each one should test their own actions. Then they can take pride in themselves alone, without comparing themselves to someone else, [5] for each one should carry their own load. [6] Nevertheless, the one who receives instruction in the word should share all good things with their instructor.

Chapter 18
Hide Your Bus in the Wash Bay! ...

One of my favorite past times when I am sitting in the lounge at the bus depot waiting for my next run for the day is to talk to other bus drivers about some of the craziest experiences they have had while driving. One driver was telling me about a friend of hers that was also a new school bus driver. When she first started driving, she had a route that was so bad that one of the parents threatened her friend and her friend got so scared that she came back to the bus depot and hid her school bus in the wash bay. She waited for an hour on her bus in the wash bay. The irate parent showed up at the bus depot with a gun in hand! The parent eventually came to her senses when the police arrived and explained to her that she was about to commit a crime that would get her locked up in jail! It rattled the driver so bad that she ended up quitting her job even though there was a police presence at the depot!

Scripture of the Day:

What does the Bible say about being afraid of people?

Proverbs 29:25 NIV

25 Fear of man will prove to be a snare, but whoever trusts in the LORD is kept safe.

A google search also explained it this way as quoted from http://Biblereasons.com

The Bible describes the fear of man in terms of a trap: "The fear of man lays a snare, but whoever trusts in the Lord is safe" (Proverbs 29:25). When we fear man, we are walking into a dangerous place, because we're no longer trusting in the Lord.

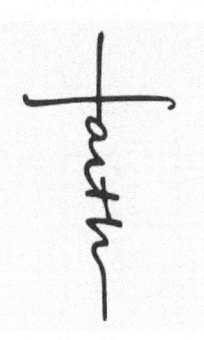

Chapter 19
Did You Pick Up Those Alibis yet?...

Hey Bus "94" Did You pick up those alibis yet? I personally don't like to call tardy or late kids Alibis. Another bus driver thought Alibi was the last name of the students missing! I had to explain to him that Alibi's was the name that was coined by another driver to give the tardy students a designated short name… Alibi is as the word sounds… Kids will always have an Alibi to explain the reason why they are late. The problem is the Career Center Shuttle bus pulls out at the exact same time every day – and we never accept any Alibis – either you are on the bus or YOU missed the bus. So, I had to explain to another driver that Alibi's meant the tardy students… I drive the "Alibi" Shuttle Bus, but I don't like the flavor of the word Alibi – so when I call in that I am about to depart I may say I have Late Arrivals from the High School I am delivering to the front door of the Career Center.

Scripture of the day:

What does scripture say about delay?

As expressed from http://www.gotquestions.org

Waiting can not only be frustrating, but it causes unnecessary stress and wasted time for the person that has to wait. Christians are exhorted by Paul to "do nothing out of selfish ambition or vain conceit, but in humility consider others better than yourselves" (Philippians 2:3). The perpetually late person does not consider others' time as more important than his own. Most habitual late-comers are concerned only with themselves. Continually being late does not communicate a zeal or diligence in serving Christ by loving others as He loves us. It also does not communicate faithfulness or trustworthiness.

Philippians 2:3 NIV

Do nothing out of selfish ambition or vain conceit. Rather, in humility value others above yourselves

Chapter 20
I Don't Care, We Are Gonna Settle This Now!...

One day an Elementary kid got on my bus barking like a dog. He had been warned repeatedly not to do so. while boarding the bus. I drove the bus about 500', pulled over, stopped, secured my bus, cut it off and stood up and I asked "Who was barking like a dog on this bus?" I let the students know I meant business… I knew who it was barking like a dog… It was Joseph! He was warned to stop as he boarded the bus but he not only ignored me, he also proceeded to do it even more and do it louder which enticed at least 2 other students to start barking too. This was the chaos I refuse to drive and put up with! So, as I asked the question... Joseph stood up and said "Yeah, it's me and you ain't gonna call me no idiot – I don't care! We are gonna settle this right here and right now!" He proceeded to stand up in a defensive position … setting the stage for something he was going to regret! I could see where this was going, and I didn't want the situation to go from bad to worst. I immediately returned to my seat and drove my bus back around the loop and took him straight to the Principal. He got off the bus and I explained to the Principal that Joseph had chosen to disobey the bus rules after repeatedly being warned to stop his unruly behavior! And so now, even worst than that behavior, he stood up in a defensive position like he wanted to fight me! The Principal kept him and made a call to his parents about his unruly behavior… The next day, the Principal discussed with me the results of that conversation with his parents. When I returned to the bus depot, I also discussed the situation with my boss in his usual calm and relaxed manner he said, "Ok I got it – Thanks for the heads up! You are doing a great job! Don't let these kids get under your skin!" The kid's bad behavior was dealt with and the next day there was no more barking from that kid. That was the end of it!

Scripture of the day:

What does Scripture say about calling someone names?

Ephesians 4:31 NIV

31 Get rid of all bitterness, rage and anger, brawling and slander, along with every form of malice.

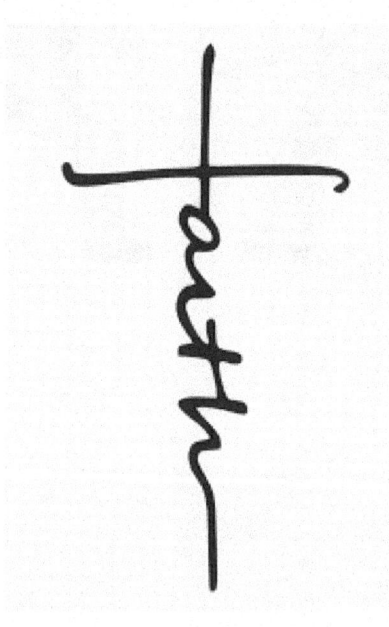

Chapter 21
An Unattended Toddler on the Curb!...

Look what I found! A one-year-old child left unattended on the curb! I need child services now! One day on the trip home I heard another driver call out for assistance. She was dropping off children in a community and somehow a toddler had wondered his/her way away from their parents and was sitting on the side of the curb, Part of our duties is to be vigilant and observant of anything that is not quite right. The driver had the right motive but it ended up as being a misunderstanding. About 10-15 minutes later she recanted but she was still very uncomfortable about the parenting skills of any parent that allows a toddler to wonder out towards the road (or even the curbside) in this matter!

Scripture of the day:

What does Scripture say about abandoned children?

A google search took me to this web site: http://understandingthebible.org and revealed…

It is clear that children are a blessing, a special reward from God. He made them wonderfully. He loves them, he longs for them to come to Him. And He is very angry when someone leads them astray.

Matthew 18:5-6 NIV

5 And whoever welcomes one such child in my name welcomes me.

6 "If anyone causes one of these little ones—those who believe in me—to stumble, it would be better for them to have a large millstone hung around their neck and to be drowned in the depths of the sea.

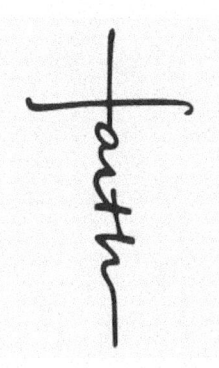

Chapter 22
Bob, Get Back to Your Seat and Sit Down!...

Elementary kids just have to talk loud, and make cat, dog, and goat sounds amongst others and stick their feet, toes, fingers, and head in twisty positions in the aisle to see what other kids are doing and to talk to them, and lay down in the seats too! Not to mention trying to move to another seat as the bus is rolling, but I have one eye on the road and one eye on them!!! So constantly every day I have to give them stern warnings like for example: "Hey Bob, get yourself back in that seat and put your shoulder against that wall! You know what my rules are so stop breaking them!"

You may be wondering why do I want them against the wall? Well, the thought behind that move is to keep kids away from the child sitting across from them; thereby minimizing the interaction between them (hopefully limiting the chaos) It also is a safety measure to safeguard any harm that may come to them from sitting near the aisle where they could potentially get hurt should I have the need to slam on brakes.

Scripture of the day:

What does Scripture say about having patience to endure stressful situations?

Isaiah 41:10-11 NIV

10 So do not fear, for I am with you; do not be dismayed, for I am your God. I will strengthen you and help you; I will uphold you with my righteous right hand.11 "All who rage against you will surely be ashamed and disgraced; those who oppose you will be as nothing and perish.

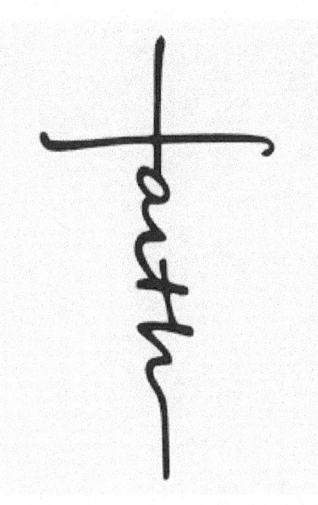

Chapter 23
Pluck Out Those Weeds, Smell Those Roses!...

Hey Jonah, I missed you yesterday! What happened? I got in a fight... I got tired of hearing that kid's sorry mouth, so I popped him one and now let's see him talk about me again! I replied to him (in my caring bus driver voice (and yes, he was a High School student!) Dang! Well, sometimes when you get backed into a corner you have no choice but to be a man and once you have given him up to 3 chances then you have a solid alibi to stand on because you have warned him. I certainly do not condone violence, but I admire a person who stands their ground! And for the short period of time, I have known you, I see a lot of good inside you! So let me tell you a story that happened to me when I was married. A man related to my former wife and I were having a conversation one day. I had a lot on my mind and he really gave me some good advice that has always stuck in my mind! He said, " Just look on that negative event as a weed in the garden of life and in any garden, you pluck out the weeds to enjoy the true goodness that's there within yourself. Don't let those weeds choke out your goodness!" So, the last two days were bad days for you, so just pluck out those weeds; forget about them and move on with the good I see in your life! Ever since that 2-minute conversation when he got on or off my bus, he was always very kind and we always enjoyed that "trademark" fist bump I always give to all of my students both boarding the bus and exiting the bus! In fact, one week I think I had a lot on my mind and one of my High School girls (not from my normal route but a Career Center student that road my shuttle bus) asked me Hey Bus-driver, why did you stop giving us fist-bumps? I told her no reason, what's your name? She said Matilda. So, I smiled and said ok, forever fist-bumps for you! She had a big glow and a smile every time we did a fist-bump the remainder of the school year!

Scripture of the day:

What does Scripture say about bad things that happen to you?

Romans 8:28 NIV.

28 And we know that in all things God works for the good of those who love him, who have been called according to his purpose.

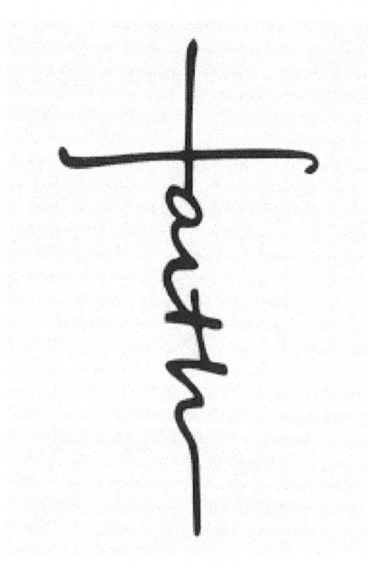

Chapter 24
You Are Going To Become A School Teacher!...

Betty, I believe in my heart that God told me you will be an Elementary School Teacher when you grow up, and quite possibly even at this very school one day. She was a fifth grader. She was a large sized fifth grader and some days she had a tendency to be a bit of a bully towards other kids! But this particular day, I happened to notice a sweeter and softer side of her. She was asking a younger kid how her day was going and she was being very sweet and kind to the kid. She smiled at the kid I could recognize that she and I shared a common trait from God and that is a genuine sense of empathy for others I told her to come to the front of the bus one day while we were waiting to off load the students because I had pulled up to the school about 5 minutes too early. There have been some days that I had to growl at her about being in her seat and moving to another seat without permission, and just the typical unruly stuff elementary kids do. But The Lord spoke to my heart on this particular day and I smiled and I said to myself, Ok God, I will be sure to tell her what you just told me! So, Betty was a bit puzzled when I asked her to come to the front of the bus. I asked her if she knew I was watching her? She said, well not really, Why were you watching me? I told her that I saw her sweet interactions with some of the younger kids. It reminded me of a school teacher and that God spoke to my heart and told me to tell you that you just may become an Elementary School teacher because you have a sweet empathetic side to you. You seem to have a caring attitude and these younger kids really look up to you! From that day forward I never had any more problems of her trying to be a bully on my bus… I hope that possibly that is all the inspiration she needs – maybe I planted a seed to inspire her to become a school teacher – who knows?

Scripture of the Day:

What does Scripture say about having empathy for others?
A google search about common questions people have revealed this…

#1. What is the spiritual gift of empathy?

It is **the ability to step into another person's shoes and understand.** Through empathy, we aim to understand what others are feeling and use this understanding to guide our thoughts and actions.

#2. Ephesians 4:29 NIV

29 Do not let any unwholesome talk come out of your mouths, but only what is helpful for building others up according to their needs, that it may benefit those who listen.

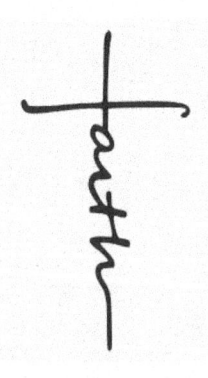

Chapter 25
That Cute Dimpled Smile…

"Gavin quit playing with that ball back there in the back seat! If you don't stop knocking that ball with that paddle and put it away or it's mine." I stopped to let Madera off the bus and in the process, Kelvin was talking loudly. I told Kelvin to move to the seat behind me, but as I walked to the rear of the bus to take away the Ball and Paddle from Gavin. I noticed Cain was playing with a yo-yo! I told him to put it away and asked did he not hear what I told him at the front of the bus? He was at the rear of the bus and since the ac is loud in the bus, I decided to give him the benefit of the doubt and told him to put it away! Meanwhile, I noticed 3 other kids either laying in the seat or having legs or feet in the aisle. I warned then and asked why they were not against the wall at the window (my way of keeping them out if the aisles). One girl Graily, smiled really big with that cute dimpled smile and confessed! She was so sweet with that little smile it just melted my heart away! I told her ok now, you know the rules! Don't break them anymore and she just kept on smiling!

Scripture of the day:

What does Scripture say about smiling?

Proverbs 15:13-15 NIV

13 A happy heart makes the face cheerful, but heartache crushes the spirit. 14 The discerning heart seeks knowledge, but the mouth of a fool feeds on folly. 15 All the days of the oppressed are wretched, but the cheerful heart has a continual feast.

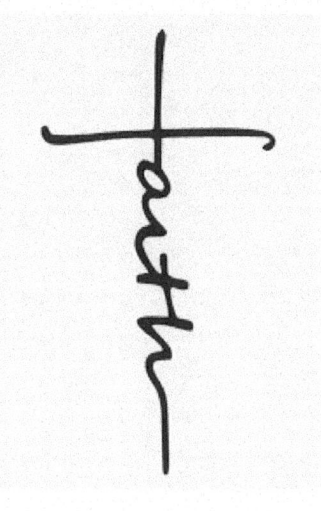

Chapter 26
Slamming the Brakes Hurt My Kneecaps! ...

Peggy was once again loud and unruly and Benny had no volume control and they got into a shouting match. I told them to get quiet. They did not pay me any attention so I pressed the brakes a little hard and everyone slightly lunged forward. It got their attention and I told them if they don't follow the rules they could get hurt. Peggy, took it literal in that she lied to her mother and claimed I slammed on brakes and she hurt her knees! Fortunately, we have cameras on the bus and also fortunately they were working and recording everything. The mom threatened to sue for medical bills if they had to go to the doctor, but after seeing the episode on the camera, she said Oh my God, is that all there was to it? I'm going home to cut that little girl's tail since she lied to me!" In the process of looking at the cameras you could clearly see the kids misbehaving and moving in and out of their seats! Upon viewing the video further, we discovered one little girl who was the oldest (and I thought my best behaved) student on the bus was "flipping the bird" at me with both hands, hiding it behind the seat in front of her! The next day I discussed with her about our camera discovery! I told her how I used to think a lot of her sweet personality and that I had a high regard for her being a leader that other kids looked up to. But all that has now changed! She dropped her head in shame. I told her I knew she was a good person and she had good inside her and her actions are observed by the younger kids. She took what I said to heart and eventually over time she grew to respect me and became a model student!

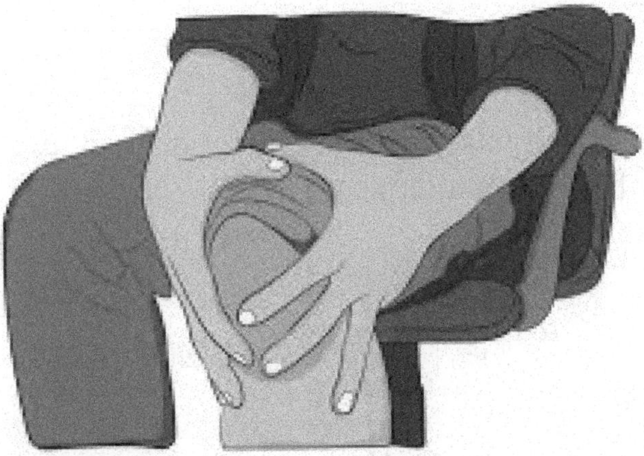

Scripture of the day:

What does Scriptures say about lying?

Ephesians 4:25 NIV

25 Therefore each of you must put off falsehood and speak truthfully to your neighbor, for we are all members of one body.

Exodus 23:1 NIV

1 "Do not spread false reports. Do not help a guilty person by being a malicious witness.

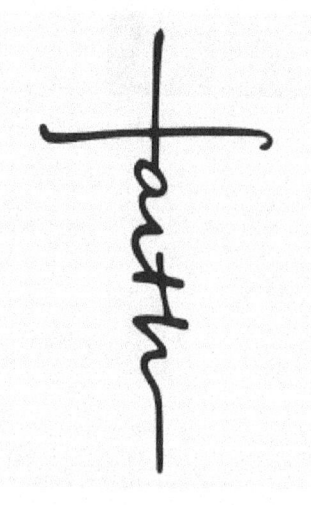

Chapter 27
Don't Tell God His Breath Stinks!...

One day on the trip home one student told another student- Donald your breath stanks! Of course, Donald had to retaliate, so I told them if they couldn't say something nice to each other then don't say anything at all! Then I asked the kids… who created you? Some of the Smart Alec kids said my momma and my daddy. Then I told them yes but who created them? Then they said their mommas and their daddies, but then I said, ok but ultimately would you not agree that we were all created by God when he created the first man (Adam) and the first woman (Eve)? They agreed. So, then I told them, well when God created man, didn't he create man in his image… right? They all agreed! So, if that's the case and you tell someone their breath stanks… aren't you essentially telling God his breath stanks because we are ultimately HIS creation(s) from the beginning of time? So, when you tell a friend that their breath stinks or you say anything mean towards them – and since we are ALL God's creation, then you are telling God himself that HIS breath stinks – Now do you think you would really want to say that to him? He could strike you down dead with a lightning bolt if he did not love you. So the next time you start to call someone a bad name or point out a person's flaws consider what God would do to you or say to you if you were saying that to him!

Scripture of the day:

What does Scripture say about demeaning other people? A google search took me to this website: https://www.pbs.org/faithandreason/theogloss/imago-body.html

The term has its roots in Genesis 1:27, wherein "God created man in his own image. . ." This scriptural passage does not mean that God is in human form, but rather, that humans are in the image of God in their moral, spiritual, and intellectual nature.

Genesis 1:27 NIV

27 So God created mankind in his own image, in the image of God he created them; male and female he created them.

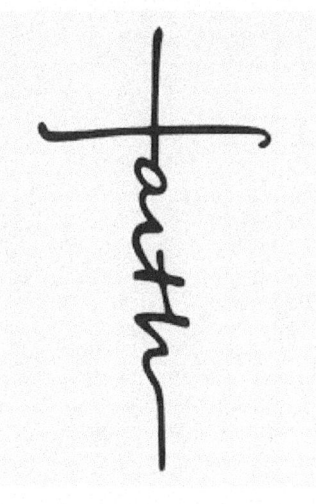

Chapter 28
The Spider Bite Parable…

This is a short story I like to call "The spider bite parable". One day a girl was being mean (or so I thought) to another girl on the bus. I told her she should be careful what she says to other people and always try to be kind. To my amazement, she asked me, well what if we are only joking to that person. I told her, well we should be kind to other people and not mean even if we are playing. We don't have that other person's brain and we have no way to know what they are thinking when we say something to them. It can be taken the wrong way by them. So, I proceeded to explain the parable of the spider bite. True story! A spider bit me on my belly. At the time, I didn't take it to be serious and therefore did nothing. But it grew into an infected area the size of a silver dollar and got infected because of neglect. It's the same way when we speak ill towards someone. That is nothing but venomous poison! Which, when we retaliate it grows and festers into more poison! But if we are kind and do good for others… it is like taking care of that spider bite… its just like putting antibiotic cream on the poison, and treating the infection!

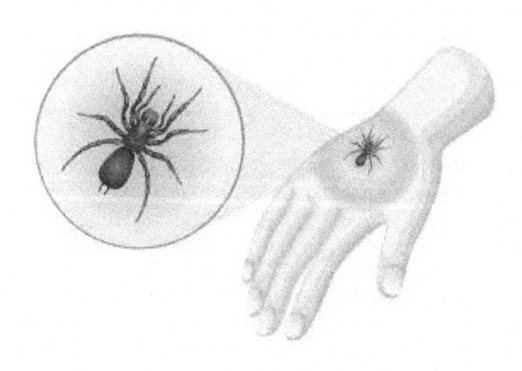

Scripture of the day:

What does Scripture say about how to deal with mean people?

A google search took me to this website: https://www.geneva.edu/blog/faith/dealing-with-challenging-people

Even if sometimes you pray through gritted teeth with clenched fists, try to call upon this piece of scripture!...

Matthew 5:43-45 NIV

43 "You have heard that it was said, 'Love your neighbor and hate your enemy.' 44 But I tell you, love your enemies and pray for those who persecute you, 45 that you may be children of your Father in heaven.

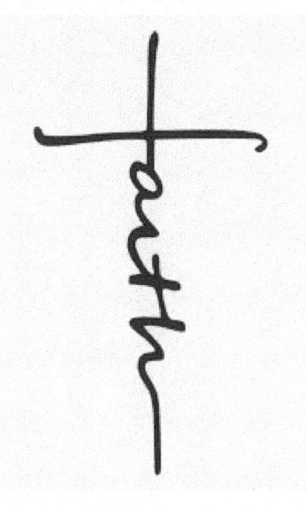

Chapter 29
The Man that Owed 10,000 talents…

We should forgive other people. It's like the parable of the man who owed 10,000 talents. The debtor expected him to pay up or go to jail! He pleaded oh no please forgive my debt, I'll get it caught up soon! So, the man's debt was forgiven… but then that same man went to another person who only owed him 100 talents (very small amount) and told him to pay up or go to jail. How can we expect God to forgive our debt and sin if we are not willing to forgive others who sin against us? Forgive us our debt as we forgive our debtors!!!! So, I need to seek out people I have been angry with and ask their forgiveness before I can expect God to intervene and forgive ME of MY shortcomings! And one last thought on the matter… Why would God allow us to take care of or do big responsibilities in heaven if we did not have the courage to listen and trust him to act upon and have faith in him to do big responsibilities here on this earth?

Scripture of the day:

What does Scripture say about asking for forgiveness when you do not forgive others who have wronged you in some way?

This brings to mind the parable of the unmerciful servant...

Matthew 18:23-35 NIV

23 "Therefore, the kingdom of heaven is like a king who wanted to settle accounts with his servants. 24 As he began the settlement, a man who owed him ten thousand bags of gold[b] was brought to him. 25 Since he was not able to pay, the master ordered that he and his wife and his children and all that he had be sold to repay the debt. 26 "At this the servant fell on his knees before him. 'Be patient with me,' he begged, 'and I will pay back everything.' 27 The servant's master took pity on him, canceled the debt and let him go. 28 "But when that servant went out, he found one of his fellow servants who owed him a hundred silver coins.[c] He grabbed him and began to choke him. 'Pay back what you owe me!' he demanded. 29 "His fellow servant fell to his knees and begged him, 'Be patient with me, and I will pay it back.' 30 "But he refused. Instead, he went off and had the man thrown into prison until he could pay the debt. 31 When the other servants saw what had happened, they were

outraged and went and told their master everything that had happened. 32 "Then the master called the servant in. 'You wicked servant,' he said, 'I canceled all that debt of yours because you begged me to. 33 Shouldn't you have had mercy on your fellow servant just as I had on you?' 34 In anger his master handed him over to the jailers to be tortured, until he should pay back all he owed. 35 "This is how my heavenly Father will treat each of you unless you forgive your brother or sister from your heart.

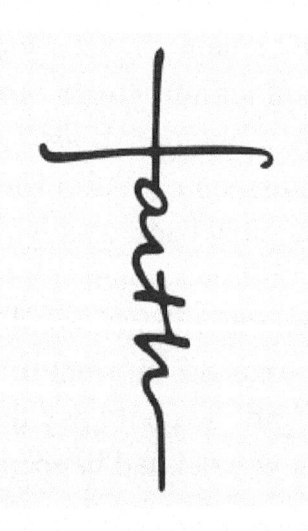

Chapter 30
I Give You a Piece of Me And A Prayer…

One thing I always like to do on my bus both when the students enter the bus and when they leave the bus, is to give them a fist bump! One day, I explained to my students what my intentions are with the fist bump… I put my fist up as you are leaving my bus at the start of the day, and when I do this action, I am giving you a little part of me to take with you… and a small prayer on my part that God will watch over you and keep you safe… I respect your individuality and it's always up to YOU whether you choose to accept my free gift or not… I respect your decision! And likewise at the end of the day as you get off my bus a similar situation. My fist goes up for you to do another fist bump… and that is also yet another prayer offered in your behalf that God will watch over you and protect you throughout the evening hours, while you are at home until the next time I pick you up!

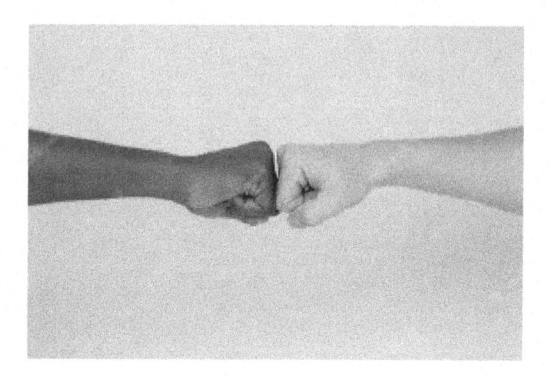

Scripture of the day:

What does Scripture say about caring for children's safety and overall goodwill?

Psalm 91:10-12 NIV

10 No harm will overtake you, no disaster will come near your tent. 11 For he will command his angels concerning you to guard you in all your ways; 12 they will lift you up in their hands, so that you will not strike your foot against a stone.

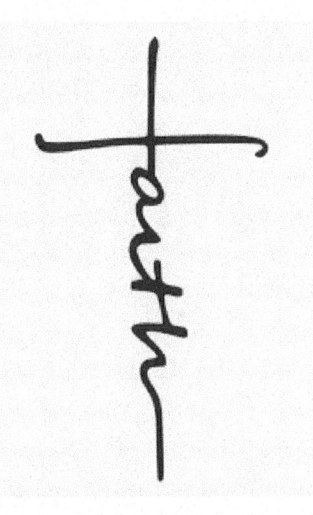

Chapter 31
Matty's Spider Bite Poison…

Matty was listening to the spider bite parable I mentioned earlier. She got so upset that as she got off the bus, she began to cry because she thought the devil was inside her and she was going to hell and she was going to burn! Petrified! I told her God would take care of her and she would be just fine! But that was the whole point of my spider bite story! I told her if you make fun of people or say something bad, it is as poisonous as a spider bite meaning you may not mean any harm! You may only mean to tease a person but if they take what you said the wrong way, then it could be devastating! Exactly like what she did! So, NOW she was feeling guilty about what she had said and now the "spider that bit her" (via her bad actions towards another child) was spreading its poisonous effects making her feel guilty of her own actions.

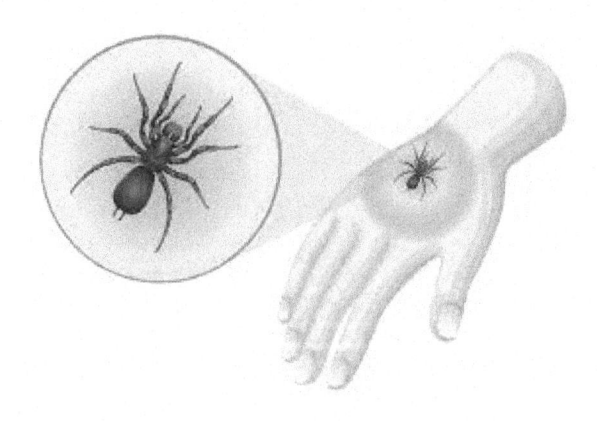

Scripture of the day:

What does Scripture say about having guilt or shame?

As quoted from a google search:

The Bible tells us we should confess our sins (1 John 1:9) and believe He has cleansed us from our guilty conscience (Hebrews 10:22). Even when someone else is responsible for bringing you shame, the scriptures urge us not to be ashamed but to glorify God instead (1 Peter 4:16).

1 John 1:9 NIV

9 If we confess our sins, he is faithful and just and will forgive us our sins and purify us from all unrighteousness.

Hebrews 10:22 NIV

22 let us draw near to God with a sincere heart and with the full assurance that faith brings, having our hearts sprinkled to cleanse us from a guilty conscience and having our bodies washed with pure water.

1 Peter 4:12-19 NIV

12 Dear friends, do not be surprised at the fiery ordeal that has come on you to test you, as though something strange were happening to you. 13 But rejoice inasmuch as you participate in the sufferings of Christ, so that you may be overjoyed when his glory is revealed. 14 If you

are insulted because of the name of Christ, you are blessed, for the Spirit of glory and of God rests on you. 15 If you suffer, it should not be as a murderer or thief or any other kind of criminal, or even as a meddler. 16 However, if you suffer as a Christian, do not be ashamed, but praise God that you bear that name. 17 For it is time for judgment to begin with God's household; and if it begins with us, what will the outcome be for those who do not obey the gospel of God? 18 And, "If it is hard for the righteous to be saved, what will become of the ungodly and the sinner?" 19 So then, those who suffer according to God's will should commit themselves to their faithful Creator and continue to do good.

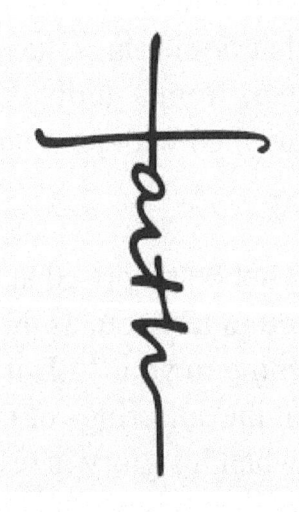

Chapter 32
Who's the B*t*h now, B*t*h?...

At Middle School, another bus driver colleague was telling me about her granddaughter who was being harassed by another boy at her school. He was calling her names like… "B*t*h, Whore, Slut, and also physically threatening her too by saying things like "I'm gonna fight you and put you down!" One day my bus driver colleague was on break and she had a big smile on her face. I asked her why was she in such a good mood. She said I am so proud of my granddaughter for standing her ground! Her granddaughter had taken all she could stand. So, one day when this bully least expected it, She threw her laptop as hard as she could at his face and it clipped his nose and broke his glasses and he started bleeding. Then she replied to him… "Now who's the b*t*h? B*T*H" He never spoke to her or harassed her ever again!

Scripture of the day:

What does Scripture say about fighting?

Romans 12:17-21 NIV

17 Do not repay anyone evil for evil. Be careful to do what is right in the eyes of everyone. 18 If it is possible, as far as it depends on you, live at peace with everyone. 19 Do not take revenge, my dear friends, but leave room for God's wrath, for it is written: "It is mine to avenge; I will repay," says the Lord. 20 On the contrary: "If your enemy is hungry, feed him; if he is thirsty, give him something to drink. In doing this, you will heap burning coals on his head." 21 Do not be overcome by evil, but overcome evil with good.

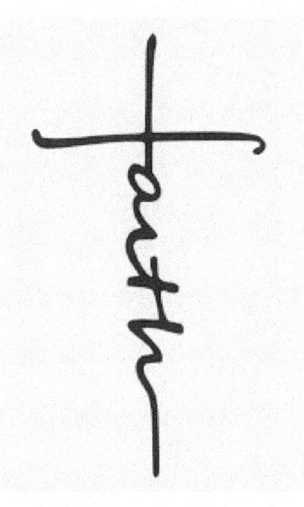

Chapter 33
Decisions You Make Today, Affects Your Future...

As I was driving my usual shuttle from the High School across town to the Career Center, I had just turned out of the bus loop when I noticed five students running on a trail beside the road away from the school parallel with the road. The trail led to somewhere under the bridge I was about to cross over. To my surprise, I knew two of the girls because they were my high school students that rode on my afternoon route. The two girls were running up that same trail. I was so disappointed because I have always had a high regard for those students! I called an official who tossed it back on my shoulders for me to tell the principal at the High School. The problem with that idea is that I would not return back to that high school until later in the afternoon and it needed to be dealt with immediately to catch them in the act. Once I got to my destination across town, I reported it to the principal at that school. I know for a fact Tammy (one of the 2 girls that normally rode my bus in the afternoon) was cutting school because she has ridden my shuttle bus on occasion going to her class during this same exact time So, at the very least she was cutting class! When you see 2 boys and 4 girls headed down a path away from school and under a bridge it's a guarantee they are up to no good!

Scripture of the Day:

What does Scripture say about making decisions?

Ask God for Wisdom and discernment:

James 1:2-5 NIV

2 Consider it pure joy, my brothers and sisters, whenever you face trials of many kinds, 3 because you know that the testing of your faith produces perseverance. 4 Let perseverance finish its work so that you may be mature and complete, not lacking anything. 5 If any of you lacks wisdom, you should ask God, who gives generously to all without finding fault, and it will be given to you.

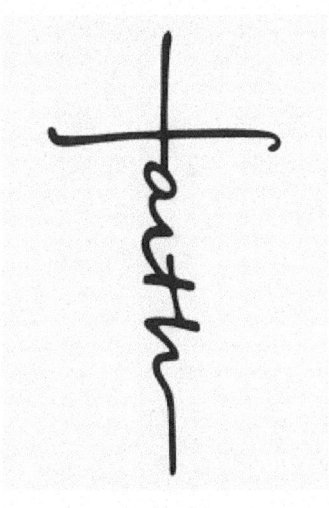

Chapter 34
Do You Still Have This Child on Your bus?...

One day I was traveling home delivering my Elementary students to their respective homes and I had a Kindergarten child on my bus. The School District is pretty strict about a policy not to allow kindergarten kids to leave your bus unless someone is there to receive them. When I arrived at his stop – no one was present to receive him – at least no one I could see. So, the child tried to leave the bus but I told him to sit back down because no one was there. The child started crying and said; but, "Why can't I get off the bus?" I explained the policy to him – but I told him don't worry, I have a few other students to deliver and then I will circle around and come right back to this same place just at the other street and they should be present then. When I came around the 2nd time – no one was present again. So, I told him I would try one more time but the protocol was always to take a student back to the school when no one was available to receive them. I delivered the other students and came back for a 3rd time and no parent was present. So, naturally, the kid was getting anxious about the situation and I drove about a block away, did a turn-about and came by his house one more time.

It's nice to know that administration is always on the ball when it comes to the safe delivery of students! I received a call across the radio from The Elementary School Principal, Dispatch, and one of my bosses wanting to know where this child was. I politely explained to them I am sitting in front of his house currently, but no one was there to receive the child! My boss asked: "Ok, What are you going to do with him, let him off the bus or take him back to the school?" I responded that I would follow protocol and deliver him back to the school. So, I took the child all the way back to the school, (as per protocol) and then dispatch called me once again wanting to know where the child was! I responded back…"Well, I am literally turning into the parking lot of the Elementary School as we speak." Dispatch responds, "Well, the parent is here at the bus depot… can you bring him back here? I responded "Sure no problem, and I delivered him back to the bus depot. Meanwhile another administration person says "That ain't gonna make you late for your end of the day Career Center to High School shuttle run is it?" I told him no worries. I pick up one single person at another high school to join the other students at the Career Center. And I was told by another driver that that student was not present on her bus earlier in the day (meaning I didn't have to maker that extra trip to pick up the High School student for the Career Center Shuttle run.) Indeed, it was not a problem… UNTIL!!! It became one! I delivered the Elementary kid to the bus depot and went back to the Career Center to pick up those kids to deliver them across town to the other High School. As those kids were getting on my bus it came over the radio that the child that I was responsible for didn't have a ride back to the High School across town! I was in a predicament! So I radioed to Dispatch that I was gonna go scoop up this other girl which would only put me 5-10 min late at the high school. Fortunately, the driver that told me she was not present on her bus earlier in the day, came to bat for me. She radioed me not to worry about picking up that student. She told me not to turn around because it would make me late at the other end. She said to just go on ahead so I could be on time, and she would pick up that girl. It made the other driver about 20 minutes late on her normal afternoon route since she picked up the slack. Later I learned that there were also two other students that she had to pick up as well which caused the long delay. Pure and simple, this was a case where another driver sacrificed time for the good of the many! I was truly grateful for her sacrifice!

Scripture of the day:

What does Scripture say about enduring a stressful job?

Matthew 11:28-30 NIV

28 "Come to me, all you who are weary and burdened, and I will give you rest. 29 Take my yoke upon you and learn from me, for I am gentle and humble in heart, and you will find rest for your souls. 30 For my yoke is easy and my burden is light."

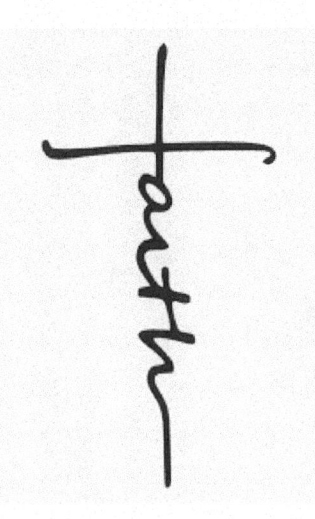

Chapter 35
Both of You Are Right And Both Are Wrong…

Angel was the one saying something derogatory to Sampson. I told both children to come up to the front of the bus and let's confront the issue and see how we could resolve the situation. I told her she needed to apologize. She did and I told Sampson now he likewise needed to apologize even if he didn't feel like apologizing because it was her fault. He had a puzzled look on his face but he apologized. I explained to them that they were BOTH right and at the same time BOTH wrong! And the funky way to fix it was to agree so that they BOTH could come back to common ground, apologize, shake hands and consider it a learning opportunity to be responsible citizens in this crazy world we have to live in and get along with each other.

Scripture of the day:

What does Scripture say about dealing with disagreements?

As expressed in http://meditate.com
Matthew chapter 18:15-16, verses 15 and 16 instructs members to **settle their differences privately with each other**. And, if this fails, they are to seek help in resolving the dispute. Moreover, if your brother sins against you, go and tell him his fault between you and him alone. If he hears you, you have gained your brother

Matthew 18:15-16 NIV

15 "If your brother or sister sins, go and point out their fault, just between the two of you. If they listen to you, you have won them over. 16 But if they will not listen, take one or two others along, so that 'every matter may be established by the testimony of two or three witnesses.'

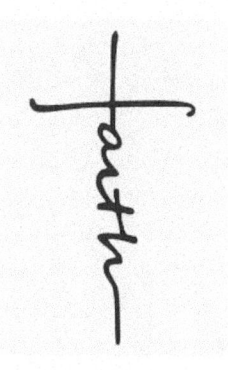

Chapter 36
The Motorcycle Thugs I Refused to Trust…

On my bus, there were two very pretty sisters that were high school students on my bus. As a driver we are supposed to always monitor safe and unsafe situations. On this particular day, at the end of the day, I dropped them off at their normal stop. At that exact time there were 2 motorcycle dudes with music blaring and engines revved up, motorcycle leathers on, and muscular. It appeared to me they were definitely up to no good. They drove past the girls and I proceeded to go on about my normal routine seeing that they drove past the girls. But I did inquire and ask them about it the next day. Both girls looked at each other and giggled and said they didn't know who the guys were. But to this day I still believe there may have been something going on!

Scripture of the day:

What does Scripture say about judging people by their outward appearances?

Luke 6:37 NIV

37 "Do not judge, and you will not be judged. Do not condemn, and you will not be condemned. Forgive, and you will be forgiven.

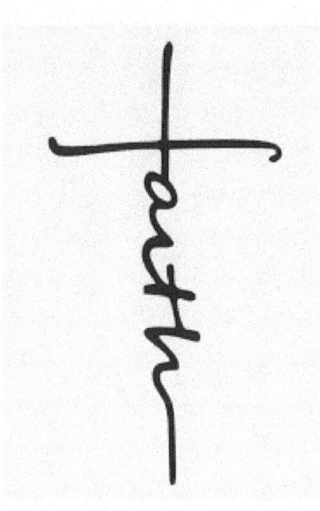

Chapter 37
Their Justification for Their Actions…

The response from those two girls about cutting school! It forever changed me! As the girls were getting off at their stop there was tension in the air! I left my door shut and spoke to them. Tammy spoke first and with this huge smile on her face she grinned and hesitantly like an innocent lamb said "Yes, we were on a school field trip today when you saw us!" But she kept smiling and never once had the slightest hint of hostility towards me! Her sister on the other hand, would not even speak or make eye contact with me and just tried to ignore me! I told both girls I needed to tell them something before they got off the bus. I told them the decisions they make especially during their high school years will have a direct impact on their future whether it be negative or positive, and they should be careful with making the right decisions on any future inappropriate situations! But, nonetheless my heart just glowed when the girl knowing full-well she and her sister were in the wrong, just smiled and seemingly (at least from her point of view) had a justifiable excuse for her actions! I was impressed at her finesse and making light of an awkward situation – seemingly making it appear to be innocent. But I'm also thankful I did my part in trying to give them good advise that hopefully would positively impact both their futures!

Scripture of the day:

What does Scripture say about being justified for our actions?

Galatians 2:16 NIV

16 know that a person is not justified by the works of the law, but by faith in Jesus Christ. So we, too, have put our faith in Christ Jesus that we may be justified by faith in Christ and not by the works of the law, because by the works of the law no one will be justified.

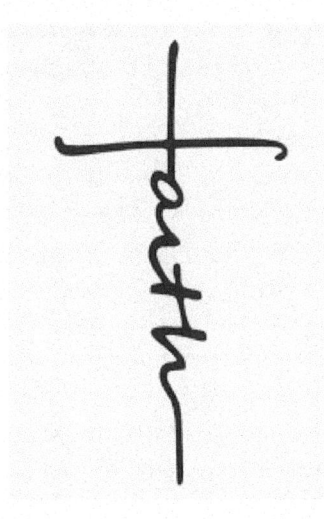

Chapter 38
The Old Tree of Wisdom and Knowledge…

One Saturday I was waiting on my dad to come and get in my car and I couldn't help but notice a radiant gold oak tree at his neighbor's house across the street. It literally looked like it was on fire. It was absolutely gorgeous. Then God spoke to my heart and made it have perspective to me. The tree was like any tree. Some leaves were old and getting dried up. But other leaves were vibrant. And it made me think of the relationship and impact my dad had on me growing up. That tree (although not fruit bearing) was in its prime leaf blooming season. Dad has always been the rock-solid tree of wisdom to me. Yes, it sways in the breeze but it is forever strong in its wisdom and producing those vibrant leaves. Then winter came and all the leaves fell off. The tree was still strong as ever but now it was transparent – naked almost. We always enjoy the beauty we always know it will bring every fall season – forever making an impact on its community. Just like my dad! Yes, 94 but always full of good wholesome Christian wisdom! Although he is retired. He presses on. He delivers meals on wheels and helps shut ins. He attends prayer breakfast and gives to the food bank. He tithes not only 10% but 20% and that is on a fixed social security income. He has always taught me God will take are of you and will always provide for your needs and then some!

Scripture of the day:

What does Scripture say about wisdom?

A google search revealed:

"Wisdom belongs to the aged, and understanding to the old," says Job 12:12, reminding us of the value of speaking with older adults. 1 Kings 12:6 tells us that Solomon once sought the expertise of older men who helped him make important decisions about the kingdom of Israel.

Job 12:12 NIV

12 Is not wisdom found among the aged? Does not long life bring understanding?

1 Kings 12:6 NIV

6 Then King Rehoboam consulted the elders who had served his father Solomon during his lifetime. "How would you advise me to answer these people?" he asked.

faith

Chapter 39
The Bully and Mother Hijacking Scene…

Well it was a crazy fiasco. My boss called over the radio asking me if everything was ok on my bus for that day? Apparently, (unbeknownst to me) a parent had called him concerned when her 2 kids had called her about the older brother being bullied on my bus. I responded yes, I am not aware of any such situation because all seems normal. Everything was so quiet you could hear a pin drop! There were never any fists or loud shouting or anything whatsoever to indicate a fight or bullying taking place. Apparently, there was a developing situation I was unaware of. The kids that were complaining about being bullied got off at the same stop as the person they were accusing of doing the bullying! Eventually, that afternoon there was a shouting match as the kids were about to get off the bus. This warranted me to stop the bus to prevent a potential escalation into a possible fight. The kid that was supposedly being bullied got off the bus immediately and ran to his house about 3 houses down the street. The kid that supposedly was the one doing the bullying was about to get off the bus, when the 1st kid's younger sister shouted out that the other kid allegedly had said he would cut him! His younger sister said she had proof on her phone that he said it! I allowed the boy (the bully) to get off the bus simply because it was his normal stop, he had to exit the bus anyway. Meanwhile, the sister is still trying to defend her brother who just jumped off the bus and left his sister behind. She was in a crying tirade and refused to exit the bus until her mother came to get her. Her mother drives up, slamming on breaks in front of the bus. She then jumps out of the car screaming for the girl to get in the car... meanwhile a crowd starts to gather because cars are now being backed up behind the bus since she has me blocked from going forward! I opened the door to see what the mother has to say and she screams to me that I'm (the driver) to blame and I should know that this behavior is happening on the bus! At this point I could tell the situation was about to escalate even worse and wisdom (maybe even God at that point) intervened. I figured, if I close the door and call Dispatch to report it, maybe the situation will be diffused at least a little bit. I was still very nervous on the bus and at this point now kids are calling their parents to come get them off the bus! I chose not to move another inch until My Supervisor arrives along with the cops to diffuse the situation! My boss took a picture of the parent's car that was blocking me along with the license plate! He told the lady to move and told me to take the rest of the kids on home, like it was a normal day. I had released one girl to her mom, then another kid was about to do the same until my Supervisor told me to not let any other kids off the bus until the students were delivered at their normal drop off points. Eventually, the parent moved her vehicle, traffic dispersed, and I proceeded to finish delivering the rest of the kids like a normal day.

175

Scripture of the day:

What does Scripture say about people who are bullied?

To Those Who Are Bullied....God Is for You!

Deuteronomy 31:6 NIV

6 Be strong and courageous. Do not be afraid or terrified because of them, for the Lord your God goes with you; he will never leave you nor forsake you."

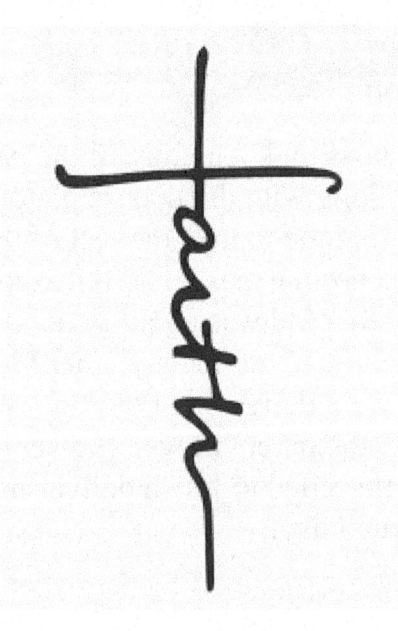

Chapter 40
Texting While Driving Cost Me $$$...

Sometimes lessons in life are hard and hard on you to learn from them! You shouldn't look at your phone and drive! While driving my personal vehicle (not the bus), I hit the curb and bent the rim on my car and blew out the tire. I managed to pull over at a gas station about a mile further down the road. The quickest thing to do was to buy a can of fix a flat. But the store price gouged me on the "only" can of "fix a flat" they had on the shelf... It was marked at $6.95 at the shelf. But when the clerk scanned the barcode on the can that 6.95 somehow became $13.95! plus pay tax on top of that! Then I had to use their air twice to try to get my tire pumped up because the fix-a-flat was not apparently working! So, I also got gouged at the air pump because it cost me $2.00 each time I used it. None of my efforts worked because unbeknownst to me I had ripped a 6" long tear in my rim and it would no longer hold air! So, my last resort was to call the "Stranded motorist membership service" to come fix it. About an hour later I get a call that the technician is delayed putting me at 9:00 pm before he can even get there to start the service repair, then once that repair is finished, I still have to travel to my hometown 45 minutes away and get up at 4:15 a.m. the next day to get ready for the workday. So, the "Stranded motorist membership service" sends out a guy who doesn't really have all the tools he needs to do the job! We needed a simple Allen wrench to take off the center cap to get to the lugs. As a "Hail Mary" pass, I took a stab that the gas station may have one for sale. I did not see one, and I suppose this is where God intervened and provided my need! While I was there, I noticed a man in a yellow coat purchasing a few lottery tickets. He looked like he was a Mechanic of some sort so I inquired "Excuse me sir, but would you happen to have an Allen wrench? His reply was yes I have a whole truck full of tools! I said, well it must be my lucky night. What type of work do you do? His reply was that he was a maintenance repair man whose job was to go help people broke down on the highway or interstate! About 1.5 hours later I was back on the road, not from the "Stranded motorist membership service" rookie who admitted this was only his 2nd week on the job but by using this other man's tools! He had to tell the "Stranded motorist membership service" guy to make sure he had the lugs on tight which he did not! One the last bolt was tightened, and we actually broke 3 ratchet wrenches… because "Stranded motorist membership service" didn't have a air wrench to take off the lugs and they were on the car too tight! The Guy in the yellow coast says well My normal fee is $75.00 to start with then we go up from there depending on what needs to be done when I help people on the highway. I asked if he took a debit card. He said no… cash only but there is an ATM machine over there across the lot. So I went to the ATM machine and got out $100.00 and gave it to him. Since I was a member of "Stranded motorist membership service" that mechanics fee was free. The other "Stranded motorist membership service" dude said, well this is actually just my 2nd week at this job. He didn't have proper tools from the get go! He had to google how to get to the tool to remove the spare tire under my car but the kicker is not only did he not tighten my lugs on the wheel enough, He left part of the wench under the car where the spare tire was dangling which was shooting sparks around my gas tank the entire 45-minute drive home. About 3 days later the tire literally was vibrating off the car and I had to pay another $300.00 to another mechanic at home to purchase new lugs and fix that spare tire. I also ended up having to hire a welder to weld the crack in the rim – another $85.00 so that stupid look at my phone ended up costing me $500.00!

Scripture of the day: (indirectly but truthful!)

What does Scripture say about texting while driving?

As expressed from https://ryanvanderland.wordpress.com

Texting while driving is, not only potentially against the law, it is actually indeed a sin. Wait! There's nothing in the Bible about texting while driving, how can I call it a sin? Allow me explain… Sin, in it's most basic, is idolatry. Idolatry is when we place anything above God. We place pleasure above God. We place money above God. We place the desire to get our own way above God. We place ourselves above God. Texting while driving is a form of placing ourselves first. It's selfishness. It's saying, "My conversation is more important than the risk to your life." It's careless, reckless and selfish and it's saying that I am more important than anyone else who's trying to go to work, pick their kids up from school, or go to the store. It's saying that I want to do what I want, regardless of it's potential effects on others. And that is sinful.

Exodus 20:3-6 NIV

3 "You shall have no other gods before me. 4 "You shall not make for yourself an image in the form of anything in heaven above or on the earth beneath or in the waters below. 5 You shall not bow down to them or worship them; for I, the Lord your God, am a jealous God,

punishing the children for the sin of the parents to the third and fourth generation of those who hate me, 6 but showing love to a thousand generations of those who love me and keep my commandments.

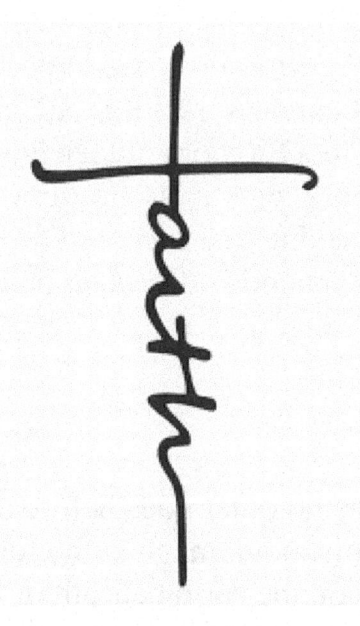

Chapter 41
Johnny Farted…

Hey Johnny farted on the bus! My response to this was: "I don't want to hear that talk on the bus now button it up." "Hey Darren, didn't your brother used to call you do-do head?" I responded: "Hush- up talk like that, but you continued on about it... I'm moving your seat to the front of the bus, Now move to seat R1 NOW!" It is absolutely astonishing what comes out of these children's mouths! I do my best to show and explain to these students what they need to do and how they should act towards one another, I try my best to teach them to live by The Golden Rule and to always be kind to others and do your best not to say hateful or derogatory things about anyone. So, the kids hate it when I say to move to seat R1 or R2. Those are the hotseats on the bus meaning I can best control their behavior(s) if they are sitting at these locations!

The GOLDEN RULE

"Do to others as you would have them do to you."

Scripture for the day:

What does Scripture say about how we should treat other people?

Matthew 7:12 NIV

12 So in everything, do to others what you would have them do to you, for this sums up the Law and the Prophets.

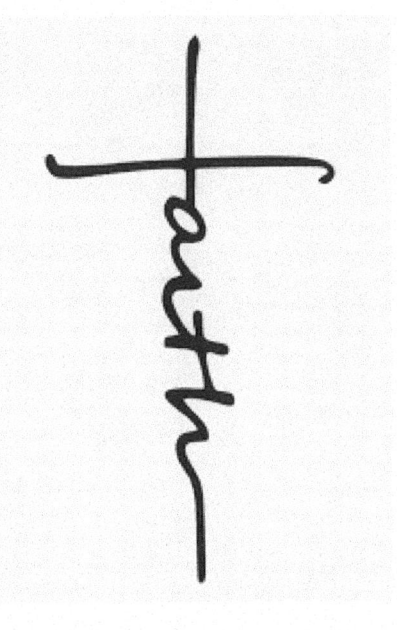

Chapter 42
My typical day starts at 4:15 am…

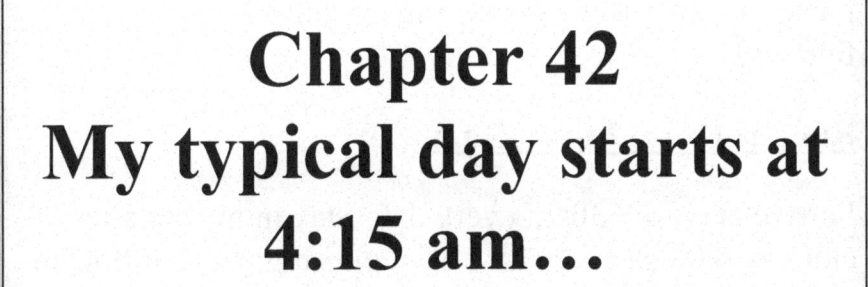

I feel certain you may like to know the typical day of a bus driver... me in particular! I normally start my day at 4:15 am. I wake up, grab a quick bath, take my old man diabetic pills, toss my clothes on, and grab 2 diet cokes out of the refrigerator just before I slip out the front door at 5:00 am. I sip on one of those diet cokes on my way traveling to the next county over from the one I live in. The trip takes about 30 minutes. I await in my car another 35-40 minutes before I can actually clock in for the day so I grab a quick snooze in my car before my day gets started.

I actually have 10 total runs throughout the day as follows:

Run #1: ES 6:22 to 7:05 am

I arrive at work 530am every day. Stay in my car and clock in 6:08ish every day. That puts my pull-out time to be 622am for my Elementary run. I leave at 6:22am on the nose, do the run arriving at ES round 6:50ish depending on traffic. ES takes in right at 7:00am.

Run #2 HS 7:06am to 8:10am

I leave at 7:05 from the Elementary School and travel across town to Sneed Rd Community for my HS run. I arrive there at Sneed Road Communty at 7:17ish. I do that run and arrive at HS at 8:05-8:10ish.

Run #3 HS TO CC Late Arrival Shuttle 8:40 -9:05

I do the late student arrival shuttle from HS to CC at 8:40am. I pull up as soon as normal CC shuttle buses leave. They leave at 8:40 am I wait 10 minutes (approved) and pull out at 8:50am. I travel to CC at get there 9:05am-9:10am-ish. So, then I wait at CC for my next Shuttle run which is at 10:00am. Since I do the late arrivals, it puts me at the very end of the fuel line on my "B" days my fuel days. By the time I wait for fueling, it's all I can do to be on time for that CC to SP shuttle run. Therefore, my solution to remedy that situation is to wait till 955am-ish at CC and pull up. Kids board around 10:10 am. I leave, do the CC to SP run and get back at 10:35 am-ish back to the bus depot. Then I go to the fuel line to get my fuel.

Mid-day (off the clock break). 10:50-1130am

Run #4 HS to CC Shuttle: 1130-1235

I clock back in at 1130 am. I then travel to HS, arriving across town at 11:45 am-ish. We then pull out at 12:05ish, travel across town to CC arriving 12:15pm-ish.

Run #5 CC to HS shuttle 12:15-12:20

I get back to the depot 12:35pm-ish. Allowing 15 min post trip puts me to clock out at 12:50pm Lunch break (off the clock) 12:50 - 1:30pm

Run #6 HS to CC shuttle 1:30-2:30

I clock in at 1:30. Arrive at HS at 1:45ish. We pull out at 2:05ish. Travel to CC arriving 2:20-2:25ish

Run #7 ES to home 2:32:3:00

I go across the street (2min) to ES and take those students home from ES. It takes 25-30 minutes to complete that run.

Run #8 HS to CC shuttle 3:00-3:22

Immediately after I finish my ES to home run #7, I go to HS to pick up a student at CC, who stays on my bus and is delivered to HS at Run #9

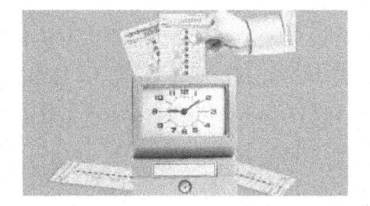

Run #9 CC to HS 3:25-3:55

I grab a load from CC and take them to HS. Students board around 3:35 and we travel back across town to HS arriving 3:55-4:00pm-ish

Run #10 HS to home. 4:00-5:15ish

We leave HS around 4:00 pm. I travel across town to Sneed Rd, Gallery Rd, Indian Arrowhead rd. areas. Usually, my normal run #10 wraps up at 4:45-4:50ish.

But here is the snafoo on that run. I have a kid who lives on Desitin rd. He was placed on my bus and I was told I could take him home at the end of my normal route. So, some days he does not ride and I get back to the depot 5:15pm-ish But, some days he does ride which puts me 530pm-ish clocking out. And another kid that lives across the street from the depot that lived on Givens Street. So, if both kids are on the bus I'm back at 530ish. But if they don't ride it's 5:15ish. I always go in and clock out immediately (essentially losing 5-10 min of legal punch out time every day because I don't want to hold up any office staff waiting on me.) I clock out and grab a bite to eat putting me maybe 6:30-6:45ish travelling home, another 30 minutes travelling home puts me arriving back at my hometown at 7:00pm, but if I go to check on my 94-year old dad, that pushes me to 7:45- 8:00pm-ish getting home. 8:00-10:00pm to wind down and watch tv go to bed at 10:00 pm and get 6-1/4 hours of sleep and repeat it again for the next 4 days!

Did I mention I also draw houseplans for extra income? So If I can muster up the energy to do so, some days I even work on that but I'm always careful not to overdo it and be too tired for work the next day. Most days I push the house plan drawings to a Saturday when I have more personal time – unless my daughter is visiting for the weekend!

Scripture of the day:

What does Scripture say about having time to do your daily routine when sometimes it seems impossible?

Philippians 4:11-13 NIV

11 I am not saying this because I am in need, for I have learned to be content whatever the circumstances. 12 I know what it is to be in need, and I know what it is to have plenty. I have learned the secret of being content in any and every situation, whether well fed or hungry, whether living in plenty or in want. 13 I can do all this through him who gives me strength.

Isaiah 40:31 NIV

31 But those who hope in the Lord will renew their strength. They will soar on wings like eagles; they will run and not grow weary, they will walk and not be faint.

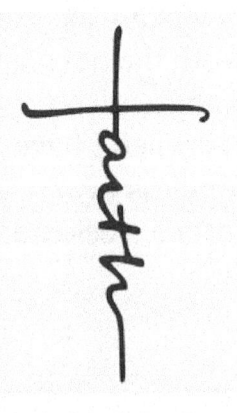

Chapter 43
Cleanup on Row 5 Seat 7 – Hand Lotion…

Cleanup row 5 seat 7! I had a student that did not show up on time for her pickup at the normal bus stop. When I pulled up to the stop, she was walking about 1/4 mile down the road from her stop. Notice I said walking – not running and basically saying by her actions that y'all are going to have to wait on me because I am not going to hurry to get on that bus! I did my normal procedures, then pulled away and left her behind! Five other students at that same stop were already waiting at the stop like she was also supposed to be doing. In 60 seconds they had boarded the bus and were already loaded. I don't wait for stroller lollygaggers! My rule of thumb is they have 5 seconds after I do my normal stopping procedures to make an effort to get on the bus. If no decent effort is being made, I leave. Sometimes these kids take me the driver for granted and don't think I will leave them. So, I left her! The next day, she (or some female student) decides to pour "Jergen's white greasy hand lotion" all out in the floor which got trampled in students' feet as they were exiting the bus. It got in the grooves of the aisle and I had to clean up that mess! I am a firm believer in karma and I believe karma will catch up with you in the future! …Or whoever poured it! But sometimes you gotta make an example out of someone so the kids know you mean business. Whether she actually poured it out, or not, is unclear but she did report to me that there was a mess in the floor… So, it appears to me it was her and she inadvertently told on herself!

194

Scripture of the day:

What does Scripture say about cleanliness?

Ezekial 36:25-27 NIV

25 I will sprinkle clean water on you, and you will be clean; I will cleanse you from all your impurities and from all your idols. 26 I will give you a new heart and put a new spirit in you; I will remove from you your heart of stone and give you a heart of flesh. 27 And I will put my Spirit in you and move you to follow my decrees and be careful to keep my laws.

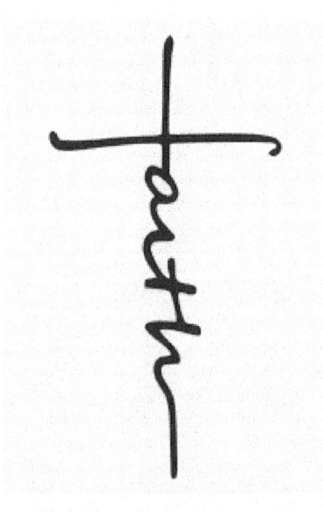

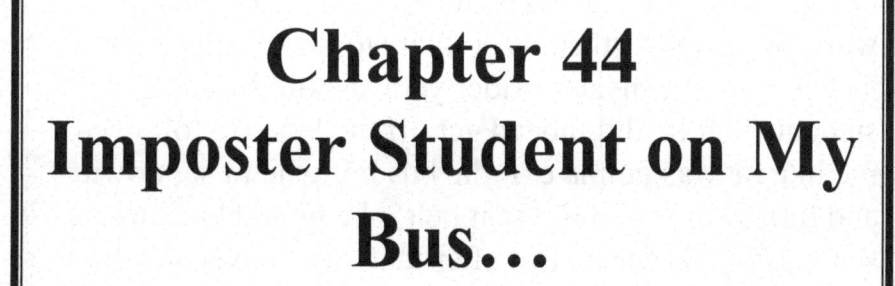

Chapter 44
Imposter Student on My Bus…

Imposter student… One day a student jumped on my bus and had their head covered. Her sister said oh that is a family member and she needs a ride home! Well, I watch closely and I know all the sheep that are in my fold. So, I always keep tabs on who rides and who is not supposed to ride my bus at all times. Well Peggy has a brother, Bobby, who is as sneaky as a snake! He was hiding in that coat. To this day I'm not sure how it worked out, but that kid did ride the bus home and I'm 99% sure it was her brother! All other buses were pulling off, so it was time for me to get seated and pull off too because if I didn't the other buses behind me would be held up! Anyway, I told Bobby to get off the bus because he was not legal! I checked the bus twice but somehow when they got off the bus at their stop, I saw the same jacket from the mystery rider yet was told by other students that he did indeed get off the bus. He followed me like he was gonna exit the bus but when I sat down and turned to fasten my seat belt – he bolted back to the seat beside his sister! But after that day I never saw him again!

Scripture of the day:

What does Scripture say about imposters?

2 Timothy 3:13-17 NIV

13 while evildoers and impostors will go from bad to worse, deceiving and being deceived. 14 But as for you, continue in what you have learned and have become convinced of, because you know those from whom you learned it, 15 and how from infancy you have known the Holy Scriptures, which are able to make you wise for salvation through faith in Christ Jesus. 16 All Scripture is God-breathed and is useful for teaching, rebuking, correcting and training in righteousness, 17 so that the servant of God may be thoroughly equipped for every good work.

Chapter 45
Poke Out Lips Girl…

If your lips were boards, I could walk from here to your house on them! One day I was taking elementary kids home and they were being their typical selves and being noisy and unruly! So, I made some of them move their seats and not be able to sit with their friends! Suzy started grumbling and complaining about me being mean to them! She was pouting with her lips poked way out of her mouth and I made the comment "Why Suzy, if your lips were boards I could walk to your house from here because you have them poked out so far!" One of her friends (whom I had told could not sit beside her) piped up at me and said: Look, you made her cry! You are just mean!" Now after finishing the elementary route for the day I started feeling bad about what I said to Suzy so I took it upon myself to go back to her house, park my bus and walk up to the door and speak to her grandmother explaining the situation. Her grandmother wanted me to apologize directly to her. I did apologize and asked her forgiveness. She forgave me and that was the end of that! I felt good about the whole situation… until… my boss called me over the radio wanting to know why I stopped in that community. I explained to him what happened. He said they have a community watch over there and I was about to get shot by a neighbor. A nosey neighbor called wanting to know what was going on and the boss told me to never stop in a community like that again. I should come back to the bus depot and make a phone call from there! … Just trying to make things right (at least in my opinion) and you get chastised for it!

Scripture of the day:

What does Scripture have to say about having self pitty and pouting?

A google search revealed:

If you have trouble with pouting, self-pity, or anger, ask the Lord to help you grow up!

2 Corinthians 5:17-21 NIV

17 Therefore, if anyone is in Christ, the new creation has come: The old has gone, the new is here! 18 All this is from God, who reconciled us to himself through Christ and gave us the ministry of reconciliation: 19 that God was reconciling the world to himself in Christ, not counting people's sins against them. And he has committed to us the message of reconciliation. 20 We are therefore Christ's ambassadors, as though God were making his appeal through us. We implore you on Christ's behalf: Be reconciled to God. 21 God made him who had no sin to be sin for us, so that in him we might become the righteousness of God.

Colossians 3:12 NIV

12 Therefore, as God's chosen people, holy and dearly loved, clothe yourselves with compassion, kindness, humility, gentleness and patience.

faith

Chapter 46
Insubordination…

Insubordination! There is always some sort of chatter on the school bus! One day I was listening in on a conversation with another driver and a school principal. Apparently, BOTH of them were having a bad day! A bus driver was telling an administrator why he left kids behind and that he refused to return to get them! The principal demanded that he come back to get them! Ultimately the administrator screamed "Sir, tomorrow after school you and me and your boss will be sitting in front of the superintendent at the district office to discuss your future employment with this district!!!" I said a prayer for him. Fortunately, he is still driving. Generally speaking, if kids are giving you bad behavior, we take them back to school and let the Administrator take them off the bus to deal with their behavior because sometimes it boils down to becoming a safety issue! Apparently, our boss eased tensions before they went to the Superintendent but I never heard any more cross words between the two of them again!

Scripture of the day:

What does Scripture say about insubordination?

A google search took me to this website:

http://www.firstcause.org/blog/insubordination

Insubordination is **the oldest recorded sin**. Lucifer resisted God's authority. He then contaminated humanity through his seditious lies to Eve. Today the planet the Lord God made for His glory is pockmarked with disobedient disregard for His rule.

Isaiah 14: 12-17 NIV

12 How you have fallen from heaven, morning star, son of the dawn! You have been cast down to the earth, you who once laid low the nations! 13 You said in your heart, "I will ascend to the heavens; I will raise my throne above the stars of God; I will sit enthroned on the mount of assembly, on the utmost heights of Mount Zaphon, 14 I will ascend above the tops of the clouds; I will make myself like the Most High." 15 But you are brought down to the realm of the dead, to the depths of the pit. 16 Those who see you stare at you, they ponder your fate: "Is this the man who shook the earth and made kingdoms tremble,17 the man who made the world a wilderness, who overthrew its cities and would not let his captives go home?"

faith

Chapter 47
Suicide...

Suicide! It came across the radio... why is that man on the side of the bridge like that? Hey he's getting ready to jump and commit suicide! Oh my god! And would you believe that when they called that out on the radio it was the exact bridge I was passing under at that exact instant. Sweet Jesus!!! I actually saw the man! I prayed... Oh please dear God don't let him jump and land in front of my bus and me run over him! Thank God the police were on the scene and were holding on to him... Driving a bus you never know what you will see on, near, or above the road, or for that matter hear on the radio! I grabbed my radio microphone and said a prayer asking God to give that man a spirit of peace in his heart and to see the better side of life than for things to be so bad for him to commit suicide. Lots of other drivers heard me and followed up with "Amen!"

Scripture of the day:

What does Scripture have to say about committing suicide?

A google search took me to this website:https://www.insightforliving.ca/read/articles/does-christian-who-commits-suicide-go-heaven

Suicide, the taking of one's own life, is ungodly because it rejects God's gift of life. No man or woman should presume to take God's authority upon themselves to end his or her own life.

Job 1:21 NIV

"Naked I came from my mother's womb, and naked I will depart. The Lord gave and the Lord has taken away; may the name of the Lord be praised."

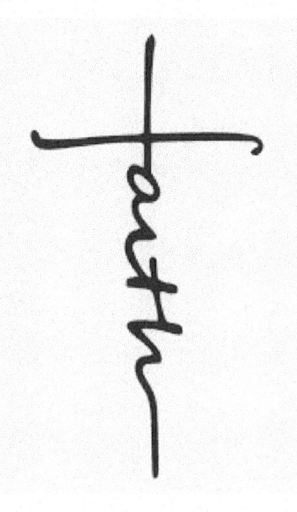

Chapter 48
Hey, KoolAid!...

Hey, Koolaid! ... You may be too young to remember. I think it was a popular commercial in the 70's. I don't especially like to hear people pick on the innocence of a Type B personality (which is a rather shy and a bit timid personality). I actually had the opportunity for this guy to ride with me on my bus to learn my route as a sub before he was assigned his main route. He was a rather shall we say big boned individual but had one of the sweetest hearts of anybody I know! From time to time, we always hear of various issues on the radio – in fact one of our requirements as a bus driver is to monitor the radio frequency, in case we forgot to pick up someone and the dispatch got a call about it and its also there for emergency situations. Traffic is often a nightmare at the end of the day. One day as I had a load of high school students and was in the process of taking them home, I was on the bus loop about to turn right onto the main road. Koolaid as they called him was about to turn into the bus loop to pick up his high school students. I take students home in the 1st wave of buses because I get there a bit quicker than other drivers since I deliver students from the Career Center to the Highschool (Other bus drivers can't depart until all Career Center students have been delivered to the High School.) Koolaid is one of the buses in the 2nd wave. He was waiting at the main road – essentially holding up traffic. Teddy bear with big brown eyes was behind him to allow the 1st wave of buses to exit. Many of the other drives said thankyou Koolaid! Of course, I got on the radio to do likewise but I called him Teddy Bear instead! I told him (and everyone – all bus drivers and all school officials out there) that since he had those big dark brown eyes and such a sweet personality and was always kind to the people and a real team – player that he reminded me of this big old Teddy Bear that a child would hug onto. Later I asked him about the nickname Koolaid – I thought their intentions were mean. He explained to me that that had always been a nickname that stuck with him because he always loved drinking Koolaid beverage when he was a child growing up and also to this very day! But when I see him holding traffic – I don't say thank you Koolaid, I say thank you Teddy Bear!

Scripture of the day:

What does Scripture say about gentle people?

A google search about common questions people also ask took me to these thoughts…

God wants us to be gentle to others. A gentle heart comes from having love for others…

Matthew 6:14-15 NIV

14 For if you forgive other people when they sin against you, your heavenly Father will also forgive you. 15 But if you do not forgive others their sins, your Father will not forgive your sins.

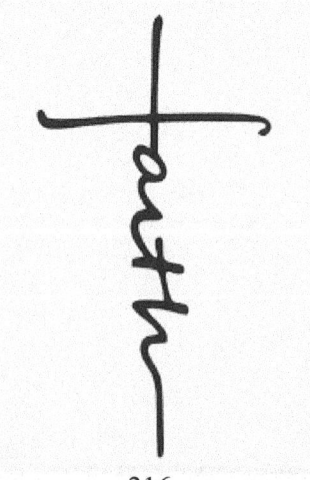

Chapter 49
It's Friday and We Shall Treat It as Such!...

It is Friday and we shall treat it as such… I think one of my most favorite endearing terms I've ever heard from a boss man is hey guys… "Today is Friday… and we will treat it as such!" So, what does that mean to the average person? Well, I think most people enjoy a Friday because after work, the weekend is here and you have a break for at least 2 days until the next work week starts! So, some people (especially towards the end of the day) like to act a fool on the radio. Me personally I enjoy saying a light hearted joke every now and again. A case in point… towards the end of my afternoon route, usually around 4:45 pm when school business is over with and done and there is minimal chatter on the radio. With radio mike in hand… I depress the call button on the mike and announce… Well fellow drivers… this is bus 94 and I'm gonna treat it as such… Here is a quick bit of humor for your Friday afternoon enjoyment. You know I am an older man. And these kids are so intelligent nowadays when they text on their phones - like all they have to do is click 2-3 letters and their friends and buddies read those 2-3 characters as an entire sentence! Ain't technology amazing – or is it the kids using that technology that's amazing? Anyway, I've been trying my best to find anyone that can tell me what these three letters mean when you text it to someone…. The letters are "I-D-K" Is there anyone out there that can tell me what I-D-K stands for? One of the other drivers told me "I don't know! … to which I responded… Exactly! Everyone out there I've ever asked tell me the same thing! I don't reckon I'll ever find anyone who knows the answer!

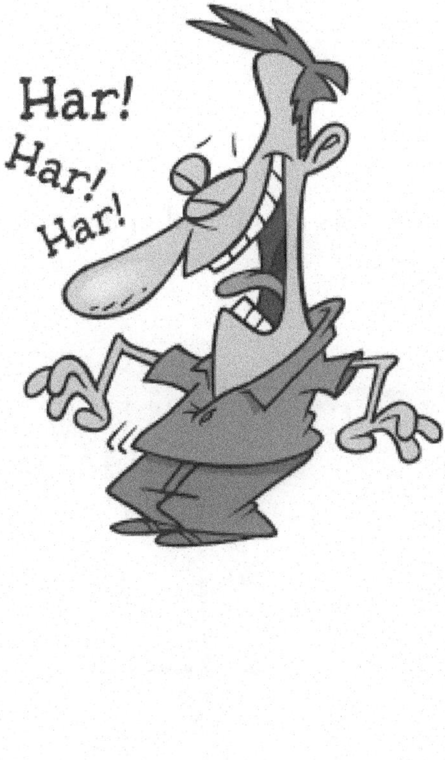
Har!
Har!
Har!

Scripture of the day:

What does Scripture have to say about laughter being good for the soul?

A google search took me to this website:

https://www.crosswalk.com/faith/bible-study/what-does-the-bible-say-about-laughter-and-its-importance.html

Laughter is a gift from God. Laughter is a great way to stay encouraged!

Proverbs 17:22 NIV.

22 A cheerful heart is good medicine, but a crushed spirit dries up the bones.

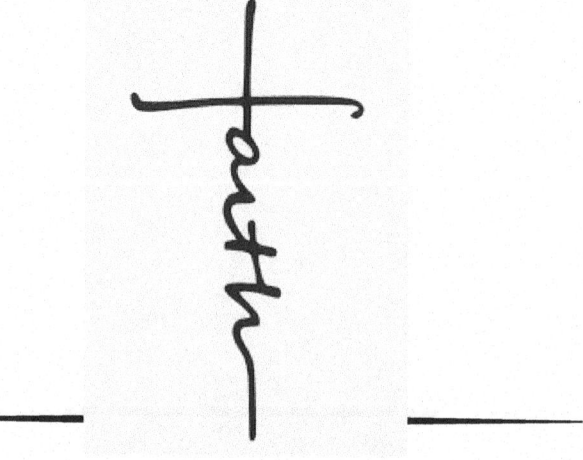

Chapter 50
Y'all Are Shining Like New Money!...

Y'all are shining like new money… There is another "catch phrase" my boss uses at the beginning of every safety meeting we have. He says now I want to tell all of you that "Yall are shining like new money" Its complimentary in his own way. It's intended to set the tone for the safety meeting because often the meeting will be to enlighten us about what we are not doing correctly so we can monitor and adjust our driving habit accordingly. One day he was explaining that sentiment in further detail. He said what is it that everybody likes, everyone can't get enough of and everyone wants? Money! Especially NEW money. So, he said it's the same way with the school district. We want you to know you are very much wanted and needed and we can't seem to get enough of it. Likewise, when you come to work on time and you do your job in spite of all the negatives you have to deal with, you are shining like new money! So, one day I was taking a mid-day break and my boss comes driving up in one of his gorgeous collector cars. He has a Shelby Mustang with a racing motor in one of his rides and he has a Plymouth (of course it is school bus yellow) Road Runner type collector cars with the bug block hemi in it. Anyway, when he drives up there are 2 things that I am impressed with… The spotless perfection of the cars he drives and also just the sound of the muscle motor and the rompety-romp-romp sound from the exhaust pipes when he backs up ever so carefully and eases into his parking spot. So, one day it was time for me to go inside to get on the clock for my next duty mid-day shuttle run. I told him, Mr. Gillicutty, I sure do like your car and you know what? You always have your rides shining like new money! He lit up like a Christmas tree with the biggest smile and he said I like that! Is everything good with you and your routes today? I respond with a Yessir. I have another question to ask you… He says "Ok – Shoot" I asked him what kind of oil do you put in those collector cars of yours to get them sounding so good with that Rompety–Romp-Romp… I want to buy some of that oil and pour it in my Escalade and see if I can get my car to sound that good! At 5:30p.m. when it was clock-out time, he saw me again and he was still smiling and passed along a positive sentiment (that is pretty much his trademark of always being upbeat, positive and always very supportive) "Thumb's up" to me!

Scripture of the day:

What does Scripture have to say about shining like new money?

It does not say "shining like new money" However indirectly it does speak of letting your light shine out to the world! When we get new money, we are proud of it and usually we have the urge to go out and spend it! In my humble opinion, this is a very close parallel to letting your Christian light shine out through your personal witness for God!

Matthew 5:14-16 NIV

14 "You are the light of the world. A town built on a hill cannot be hidden. 15 Neither do people light a lamp and put it under a bowl. Instead, they put it on its stand, and it gives light to everyone in the house. 16 In the same way, let your light shine before others, that they may see your good deeds and glorify your Father in heaven.

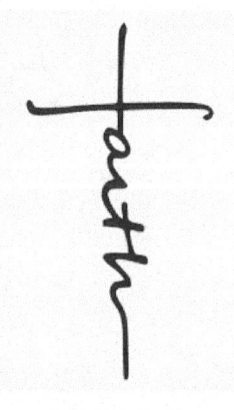

Chapter 51
Paradice!...

Paradice…We have another driver that is a cool and slick dude as I may call him. I was teasing him one day. He had many nicknames but one of his nicknames I like to call him by was Dice. I can't help but to chuckle. His bus number is 88 and he comes across the radio often saying "Ochenta is what they call me!" So, I made a little rhyme for Him… "Ochenta. Ochenta. He will always be my friend and my Menta!" I saw a picture of a set of Dice on the tag of his car one day. I was teasing him one day when I saw his two grand-children with him at work. I told him, well Dice they call you Dice, but when I see that big smile on your face when your grandchildren are around you… I think your nickname changes to "Paradise" – because your love for them shines like you are in Paradise! He spoke back to me a comment from one of my favorite movie star characters… Denzel Washington…. "My man!"

Scripture of the day:

What does Scripture say about grandchildren?

The Bible tells us that it is a blessing to have grandchildren!

Proverbs 17:6 NIV

6 Children's children are a crown to the aged, and parents are the pride of their children

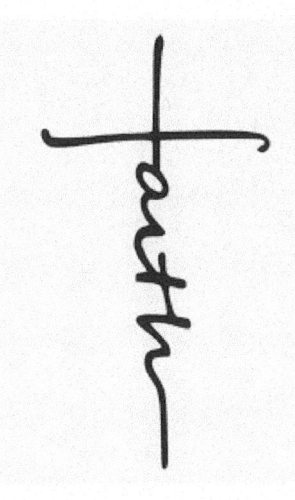

Chapter 52
Let's Get It!...

Let's get it... There is a slogan made by a popular shoe company, and they also have a swoosh logo on all of their tennis shoes. Well, one day I couldn't help but notice that every day, at the same time, my mentor would get on the radio, when it is time for all of the shuttles to depart from their respective schools and deliver their shuttle runs to their appropriate destinations his catch phrase is "Let's get it..." I started thinking wow he should market that phrase because it is so simple... yet it has tremendous impact about its core meaning. I am a very deep thinker, and I ponder about what people say – often! I also do a lot of reading. I love to read anything that will allow me to grow spiritually. Anyway, one of my readings was talking about when we do our job, how do we approach it? Do we give it everything we got and want to do it the best we can and be the best at it or do we have a lackadaisical attitude about it? The reading pointed out that somewhere in scripture, I think it was about the man who had the talents (or money) that he gave to 3 men. Two of them invested it and made their master more money and one of them buried it in a jar. When the master returned, he gave it back to him – ie; he was lazy at his job and did nothing with his talents (money) that was given to him! So, another point was made that if God puts us in charge of little things in this life here on earth and we fail at it because we are lazy, then once we get to heaven how can we expect God to give us bountiful blessing to be in charge of when we in effect wasted out talents. My point in this story is that our work ethic in whatever it is we are doing as a profession here on this earth should be delivered to its fullest potential – as if we were doing a job for God himself! So coming back full circle to my fellow bus driver's slogan – "Let's get it!" It is so simple – yet SOOO profound! Let's get it implies let's go do the work we are getting paid for and be happy with the blessings we have!... at least that is my interpretation of his slogan… "Let's get it!"

Scripture of the day:

What does Scripture have to say about working earnestly in your place of occupation?

Colossians 3:23-24 NIV

23 Whatever you do, work at it with all your heart, as working for the Lord, not for human masters, 24 since you know that you will receive an inheritance from the Lord as a reward. It is the Lord Christ you are serving.

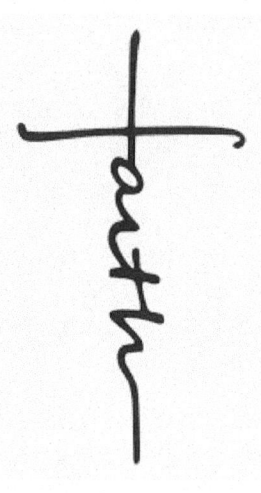

Chapter 53
Easter Eggs! ...

Easter Eggs. On the Monday after Easter one of my little kids on the Elementary School routes asked me how many eggs did I find in my easter basket? I told him I didn't go Easter egg hunting. With his sweet dark eyes and in his innocence, he says Mr Bus driver – do you mean to tell me the Easter Bunny didn't come to visit you? This brings another story in mind to me I wish to share with you… I always struggle to find meaning in most everything I do. One summer I was working with a youth ministry camp and one of the adult leaders was sharing her insight with us. She asked some of the kids at the camp… Do you like going on Easter Egg hunts when you were a child? All of the kids were teenagers at least 14 years old or older which was one of the requirements to participate in the summer mission camp. Some said yes sure – especially the girls – most of the guys just sort of shrugged their shoulders and smiled! Anyway, she said well finding God and how he is good to you and how he provides for your every need is EXACTLY like hunting for eggs in an Easter Egg hunt! One of the kids said… "Whuddaya mean?" Well, what was the whole fun part of the hunt? One of the girls said… well you could find eggs in the craziest of places! The lady exclaimed EXACTLY! That's the same way it is with God! How many eggs did you find if you didn't go out and look for them? The kids said, well None, I guess! The lady replied once again… EXACTLY! Think about it, if we never look for where God is in our lives then we miss out on all those wonderful gifts he gives to us every day… I'll bet for every single bad thing that happens in life you can discover two more good things that occurred as a result of the bad thing… maybe not immediately but if you stop and think about it (in other words if you stop and take time to notice WHERE those hidden gems of Easter eggs are at – of God's grace and blessings extended out to you, you will be amazed! But if you never take the time to look, you can never find God interweaved and intertwined throughout your life! It was a story that made a profound effect on my personal Christian life and when my Elementary kids asked me about my eggs, I couldn't help but think of that story that was revealed to me one hot summer on a mission camp in the middle of summer.

Scripture of the day:

What does Scripture have to say about seeking out hidden wisdom?

A google search took me to the following website:

http://fbcbridgeport.org/easter-eggs/

In his first letter to the Church in Corinth, the Apostle Paul encourages his readers (both then and now) to go deeper than what human reasoning can give us, seeking out a "secret and hidden" wisdom.

1 Corinthians 2:7-9 NIV

7 No, we declare God's wisdom, a mystery that has been hidden and that God destined for our glory before time began. 8 None of the rulers of this age understood it, for if they had, they would not have crucified the Lord of glory. 9 However, as it is written: "What no eye has seen, what no ear has heard, and what no human mind has conceived"— the things God has prepared for those who love him

Chapter 54
Teddy Bear's Bus Was Hi-jacked!...

My bus was hijacked this morning! One morning maybe 5 minutes before I left the bus depot, I had been on my bus for 15 minutes finishing up on my pre—ride bus checklist and was waiting for the alarm to go off on my phone for me to leave and pick up my kids to take them to Elementary School – as was my normal routine every day. I had just finished my radio check to make sure my radio was working properly when I heard Teddy Bear in a frail and nervous voice come across the radio and ask – Hey what is the procedure when someone wants to get on the bus that is a bystander. Of course, Dispatch responded "Don't let him on! Do you have students on the bus already?" Teddy Bear responded no not yet. Some guy is standing in front of my bus, the door is closed but he won't let me by until I open the door to let him on the bus! It was at this point the Safety Boss requested his location and he said "Hang tight, help is on the way – what is your location?" Teddy bear told him his location but to everyone's amazement he also responded this man is crazy! He just jumped on the hood of my bus and climbed on top and is coming into my bus through the roof vent. I'm telling ya'll right now if it comes down to it, I WILL PROTECT myself at all costs and I will not be held responsible for my actions! The "new rider" at this point told Teddy Bear that there were some people chasing him who were going to kill him and he was trying to escape! Teddy Bear was driving very slow as the situation continued to develop but police had already arrived at the scene. The

Big Boss came over the radio and said "We are on our way." He asked Teddy Bear if he had a gun. He said No not that I can tell right now. The rider then thought the people that were chasing him were coming in the back door of the bus and were going to kill him. The passenger at this point was probably seeing the blue lights of the approaching cop cars! He grabbed the fire extinguisher and sprayed it all over the bus thinking he was defending himself! After everything calmed down, the passenger was suspected of being hyped up on drugs! He eventually exited the bus with his hands up. Teddy Bear ended up being a hero for his calmness during these events and handling the situation in a professional manner but was allowed to take the rest of the day off because of the emotional stress of the situation. He ended up having to drive a spare bus for the next few days or so, so his bus could be cleaned up from the contents of what was sprayed out from that fire extinguisher!

Scripture of the day:

What does Scripture have to say about handling fearful situations?

Psalm 23:1-6 NIV

1 The Lord is my shepherd, I lack nothing. 2 He makes me lie down in green pastures, he leads me beside quiet waters, 3 He refreshes my soul. He guides me along the right paths for his name's sake. 4 Even though I walk through the darkest valley, I will fear no evil, for you are with me; your rod and your staff, they comfort me. 5 You prepare a table before me in the presence of my enemies. You anoint my head with oil; my cup overflows. 6 Surely your goodness and love will follow me all the days of my life, and I will dwell in the house of the Lord forever.

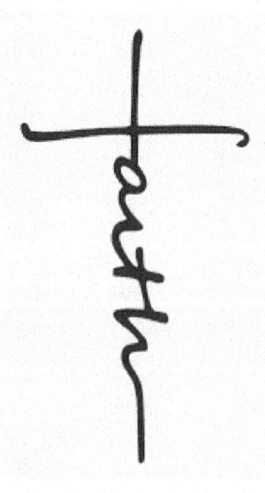

faith

Chapter 55
The Master Link…

Master link. One day we were all driving and performing our normal drop off duties and in general trying to be complementary of each other. Some drivers are very patient. Yet some drivers are just plain mean with some of their comments on the radio. One day I was pondering all the "stuff" that our dispatcher (along with the bosses above him) have to deal with on a daily basis. Maybe a driver missed a stop. Was that miss of a stop legitimate? Sometimes kids do like they are supposed to yet other times they stay in their house too long and thus parents call in saying the driver just pulled off and left them! So, Dispatch has to call and make a decision of how to get that kid to school. Sometimes it's an innocent mistake and drivers will turn around and apologize for their oversight. But sometimes the driver chooses to explain their side of the story and dispatch has to either get another driver to go by and get that kid or tell the parent that after three times if no one is there when the bus arrives, it is our policy that the driver does not have to stop. Some days for various situations that occur - the driver may have overslept, or not be able to come in at all or worst-case scenario just plain quit! Then it is dispatch's responsibility to find a way to get another driver (or sub person) to double up their route and cover for them. It makes them late for their normal duties – but its either be 30 min late getting to school and help cover that route or an entire school bus of kids not arriving at school at all. It's our job to get them to school! So, in effort to show appreciation for all that craziness they have to deal with daily – not to mention irate parents that call about little situations that happened to their child on the bus on the way to school – none of which the driver can totally prevent because they have to focus on driving. I decided one day to radio in and say that as drivers we were links in a chain like a bicycle chain. But if you don't have that "Master link" that connects that chain then the chain (and the system) is essentially useless. You can't ride that bike if you don't have a usable Master link that allows the chain to do its duty! So that name sort of stuck out in other driver's minds and from time to time I hear other drivers respond to Dispatch as being "The Master link!" Dispatch was very excited about their new name! He came across the radio after I told him that and said "Now that's what I'm talking about! You could hear the pride in his voice – it truly made my heart glow! So for me that was a real win-win for everyone!

Scripture of the day:

What does Scripture have to say about being diligent in your work?

Colossians 3:23 NIV

23 Whatever you do, work at it with all your heart, as working for the Lord, not for human masters,

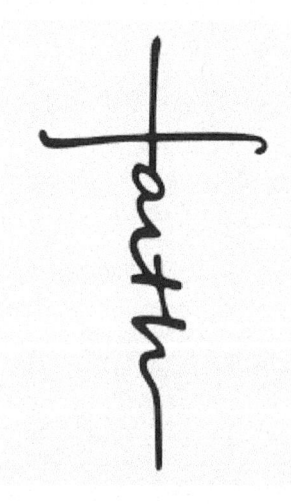

Chapter 56
The Well-Oiled Machine...

The Well-oiled machine… In the last Chapter I mentioned about the Master link… being our Dispatch person. I heard early on the radio this particular day Have y'all seen bus 38? "No" was the response "that bus is still on the yard." Then another person says I don't think bus 25 is here today either. So, the next thing you know, and this is absolutely NO lie! Our Master Link had some 25 routes that he had to find a way to get covered! I was so amazed to hear on the radio other drivers coming up to the plate to help out… "Ok I'll cover 38 when I finish my elementary run…" and another driver says well I can go back and take bus 25's elementary with my High School kids. And a few other drivers chime in well I can pick up Picket, and Blanding Court, and Highland Avenue and help out with that much of route 72. "Hey Route 87 can you get the back end of that route and between the two of us we'll get them covered!" It was absolutely amazing. Dispatch came across the radio – Today. We are gonna need help with the following routes… as I said some 25 routes (about ¼ of our work force) had to be covered. But at the end of the day somehow, some way it ALL got covered and kids were delivered (albeit – maybe a little bit later than usual) but all were delivered to and from school! I've heard my Mentor call across the radio during all the chaos that gets handled every day say "It's like a well-oiled machine!"

Scripture of the day:

What does Scripture say about working hard?

Proverbs 14:23 NIV

23 All hard work brings a profit, but mere talk leads only to poverty.

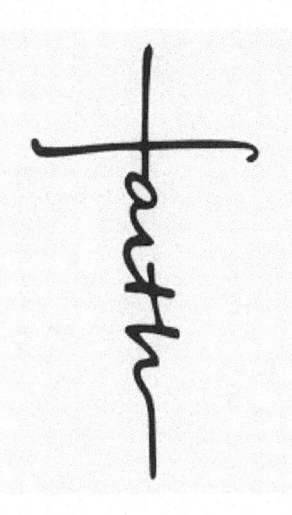

Chapter 57
Foolish Horse-Play…

El-don got on the bus in a big wave of kids pushing their way to get on the bus to get to their seat. In the process he was in an argument with Joanne and he slapped her on her face. I noticed it happen, although it wasn't a hard slap, Joanne had to make a big to-do about it and said "Hey, he slapped me!" She ended up reporting it to the Principal. He asked me about it and I said yes, I saw it but it wasn't a hard or mean slap. It was a slight tap in the confusion of all those kids boarding the bus in one wave and in all honesty, she made an attempt to slap him back. So, I made the effort to make sure we never had a wave of kids get on the bus pushing each other. El-don and Chris were running and pushing and shoving each other to get to the front of line (during the confusion of all this is when the girl got slapped). I made the two boys get off the bus and go to the rear of the bus line to board. From that day on I made sure to monitor them boarding the bus to make sure no one was pushing and shoving. I also noticed we had the same issue at arrival at school. I made the same rule… no one can push and shove and those in the back should never be the 1st ones off the bus. You need to wait for whoever is in the seat in front of you to get off the bus before you can get yourself off the bus!

Scripture of the day:

What does the Scripture say about idle horseplay?

Psalm 32:8-11 NIV

8 I will instruct you and teach you in the way you should go; I will counsel you with my loving eye on you. 9 Do not be like the horse or the mule, which have no understanding but must be controlled by bit and bridle or they will not come to you. 10 Many are the woes of the wicked, but the Lord's unfailing love surrounds the one who trusts in him. 11 Rejoice in the Lord and be glad, you righteous; sing, all you who are upright in heart!.

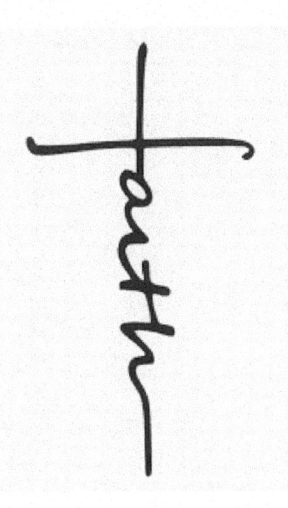

Chapter 58
Can You Say Busted?...

Can you say busted? It amazes me what kids will say sometimes! I suppose I must also consider their age and that they are still in the stages of learning from their life experiences. I have two cases in point...On two separate instances kids balled up paper and threw trash on the floor. Part of the duties and responsibilities as a bus driver is to maintain cleanliness on the bus – so I must pick-up all paper and trash and candy and wrappers and keep the bus swept. Jinny balled up her homework and tossed it at another student and on another day, Tony had a picture of a concrete mixer truck he had been coloring and he wrote his name on it... He decided he would also use it to throw at another student on the bus. So, the next day, I confronted both students about their trash throwing – both of them denied any wrongdoing! But I noticed their complexion turned to a fait tint of red when I opened up the balls of paper that was thrown on the floor the day before and it revealed their names! They still tried to deny it! I told them they were both BUSTED and whether they actually threw it or not, the papers did not magically come out of their notebooks and write their names on them by themselves. Regardless of when it was thrown it was in a place it was not supposed to be and the next time they threw paper (or balled up any kind of paper) they would not only pick it up but they would also have to clean up the entire bus. We know that there is no way I can force them to do that but part of being a bus driver is knowing when you can and when you can-not use psychology and bluff a kid! Our protocol is to do writeups to establish a written record of the history of what is occurring and if there become multiple writeups –

then there is written documentation to prove it and it's not just here-say that a child has bad behavior. Usually it only takes one write-up (two at the most) to make that inappropriate behavior stop! Not only did I do their write-ups but I also stapled the tangible evidence of the pieces of paper with their names on it so there was no denying it was theirs!

Scripture of the day:

What does Scripture say about honesty and integrity?

The entire 12th chapter of proverbs is a dance back and forth of good vs evil but Proverbs 12:22 expresses the sentiment of this chapter the best! It has always been my practice to always tell the truth and to be honest in everything you do in life. Because if you lie about something, or try to cover it up, then you have to tell another on top of another lie. It has been a painful conviction of mine to follow the ideals my parents taught me. It cost me dearly in a personal relationship and it also cost me in a career move – but in both situations, if I were to die in an instant and have to face God himself for my actions, I would be clean as a whistle. Consider your own personal convictions – do you have a clear conscience? Have you always told the truth even with the fate of having to face dire consequences?

Proverbs 12:22 NIV
22. The LORD detests lying lips, but he delights in people who are trustworthy.

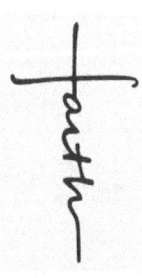

Chapter 59
The Crazy Things You Find on a Bus…

Sometimes you find the craziest things on your bus… As mentioned previously, one of the duties I am taxed with is keeping the bus clean… Generally speaking, we are supposed to sweep it off every day and maybe once or twice a week mop the floors. One day while doing my sweeping routine, I kept noticing a round puddle on the floor with a salty looking chalky substance on the floor of the rear seat. I had been keeping my eye on the situation to determine whether it was occurring from my normal bus riders or my shuttle bus riders. I went back and checked behind the rear seat after each run and narrowed it down to my High School group. I went to the back of the bus and confronted the student that sat in that particular seat. I was polite to him and told him considering the seating chart, and where the actual evidence was, it was leading me to believe that he was the person who was drooling on my bus. Of course, the kid denied it. So I told him, if I am wrongfully accusing you, then I apologize to you – but if it's you doing it please stop because I am the one that has to come behind you and clean that stuff up and it's just gross. After having that confrontation, I never saw the drooling pool of spittle again. If it wasn't that kid, then he knew who it was that was doing it. I am thankful the behavior stopped. There are other peculiar things you find when cleaning up your bus! Mostly the usual stuff – paper wrappers and, (Oh do I ever hate it when I find them…) chewing gum just spit out on the floor. I make efforts to clean it up, but by far the

258

chewing gum is the nastiest! Sometimes there are mashed up gummies. I have even found cheese mashed onto the walls that dried in place and that's hard to get off the walls. I even found skittles mashed onto the ceiling of the bus one time. Sometimes I find ear buds and headphones. On occasion I find I-phones but usually the kids miss those I-phones and head phones and come running back looking for them. Sometimes I find money. Thankfully, I have a pretty respectable group of students who ride my bus… In some situations, it's just a kid trying to do a prank of some sort to get attention. So, for the most part I try not to show any reaction to the things I find on the bus. As my dad once said "Sometimes it's best to let Sleeping dogs lie! And don't stir up any trouble needlessly"

Let sleeping dogs lie.

Scripture of the day:

What does Scripture say about keeping your work-place clean?

While researching this scripture I was actually very shocked at what I read! I totally agree with the sentiment but in all of my years of reading scriptures in the bible, Ive never read this until preparing this book!

Deuteronomy 23:12-14 NIV

12 Designate a place outside the camp where you can go to relieve yourself. 13 As part of your equipment have something to dig with, and when you relieve yourself, dig a hole and cover up your excrement. 14 For the Lord your God moves about in your camp to protect you and to deliver your enemies to you. Your camp must be holy, so that he will not see among you anything indecent and turn away from you.

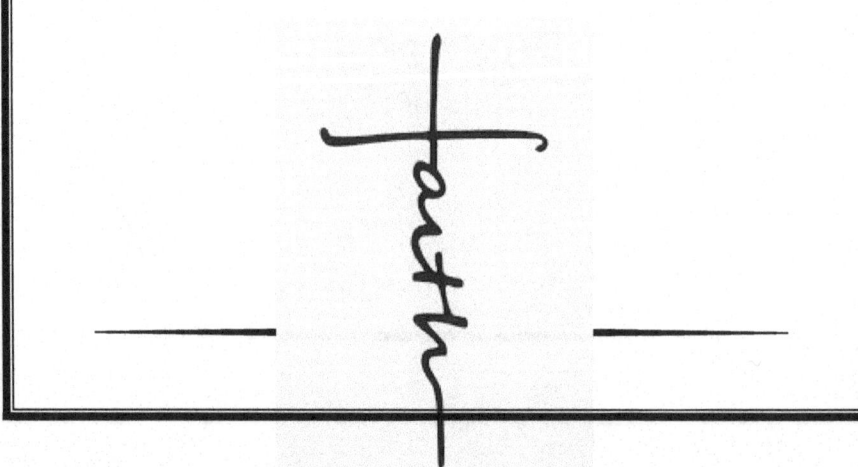

Chapter 60
The Bus I Totaled in High School!...

I believe that one of my most frightening moments I have ever experienced in my life was the bus accident I had when I was a bus driver during my High School years. To the best of my recollection – this is how it went down…I had just picked up my Elementary Kids and was traveling to the Junior High School to pick up those students. The intersection that the accident occurred at was maybe 2-3 blocks from the High School. Of course, some students (mostly seniors) had early release so some traffic was coming towards the intersection I was about to travel through. I recall a quick one second glance out my left window. I could tell it was either a Trans-Am or a Firebird and as I travelled through the intersection (I had the right of way – they had a stop sign in their direction of travel) I recall thinking they had better slow down… or "CABAM!" followed by a huge "BAM!" Screeching of tires! I recall my head hitting the pole inside the bus. It was a noticeable tap, but not a very hard hit; however, nonetheless, it was a hit. Fortunately, I was wearing my seat belt! I also recall one or two elementary kids sitting in the front seat to my right… of course one child was standing up at the time and was tossed in the stair well. The momentum of my bus going through the intersection and being hit just in front of the rear wheels of the bus pushed the trajectory of my bus between a power pole and a stop sign, consequentially running over a fire hydrant. An elderly lady was coming out of her house to the front porch that I was just about to destroy. I recall saying God please help me! … to which I know he always has and always will help me and protect me to this very day – Somehow, I just know He always hears my prayers and keeps me safe! Anyway, as God would have it, the fire hydrant remained intact – it did not pop off – had it popped off, surely it would have shot water up. I could have easily crashed into the power pole which might have easily electrocuted someone! He even protected the woman coming out on the porch! How is that even possible you might ask? Well, the front wheels were literally ripped out from under the bus by running over the fire hydrant, and the front wheels got caught by the back wheels, which made my bus become like a big bulldozer. The bumper dug into the ground only inches before hitting the house! Of course, firetrucks, police, and ambulances were all on the scene within minutes. Luckily, I had the wits about me to tell my kids to go to the rear of the bus and evacuate. They started screaming and panicking because they thought the bus was on fire (once again I believe God's angels were protecting us!) In a calm voice I told them not to worry. Yes, it's a bad accident but let's all get off the bus. I told them it was just dust stirred up that looked like smoke by the accident we were just involved in. I gathered them all together across the street out of harms way. Two kids were slightly injured with only slight cuts and scrapes but they took them to the hospital just to be sure. The car that had run the stop sign was driven by two girls that had just left the High School. Both of them were injured but they only had a broken wrist or broken arm from such a severe crash. I had become some-what of a hero and there were photos of the accident. The local newspapers showed me holding my kids at a safe distance, and there was one photo that had a picture of me looking at my bus. They described me as being a skilled bus driver and due to my skills and quick thinking, there were not as many injuries from what could have been a catastrophe. To the best of my recollection, I think I told the newspaper writers it wasn't me driving that bus. I was just holding on for dear life! God had the wheel! I wanted to be sure to give Him the praise and glory!

Scripture of the Day:

What does Scripture say about God protecting you during life threatening situations?

Psalm 91: 9-11 NIV

9 If you say, "The Lord is my refuge," and you make the Most High your dwelling,10 no harm will overtake you, no disaster will come near your tent. 11 For he will command his angels concerning you to guard you in all your ways;

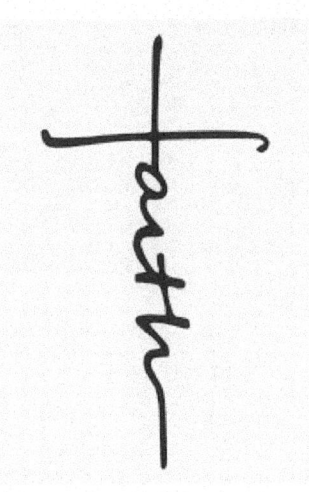

Stay Tuned! ...

Stay tuned for the next exciting volume to be published within the next year! Here are some of the enticing titles of new, comical, and fun stories coming soon! Enjoy… in the near future!

- ✓ Bus Wreck at the Railroad Tracks!
- ✓ Let Me Off This Bus Now!
- ✓ The Coin Collector!
- ✓ If You Keep Taking Drugs You Will Die!
- ✓ One Of My Worst Driving Predicaments!
- ✓ Lawsuits!
- ✓ …as well as many other funny, new, exciting, crazy, astonishing Mis-Adventures of Bus #94!